Glossary of
Cyber Warfare, Cyber Crime
Cyber Security

By

Dan Remenyi
Richard L Wilson

Glossary of Cyber warfare, Cyber Crime and Cyber Security

First Edition, June 2018

Copyright ©2018 ACPIL

First edition

ISBN: 978-1-911218-87-6 (Soft back)

Published by Academic Conferences and Journals International Limited, Reading, RG4 9SJ, United Kingdom. Printed by Lightning Source

Available from www.academic-bookshop.com

Contents

Foreword

The domain of cyberspace is a highly contested one. Attackers and defenders are engaged in an ongoing battle of wits and resources that has increasingly become a source of risk for all who ply their craft in the digital sphere. Yet, this constant battle to break, or to ensure, cyber security is not the only way in which cyberspace is contested. The language we use to describe cyberspace, to talk about activities within cyberspace, and to convey the impact of effects enabled by activities in cyberspace, also provides a field of battle.

Scholars and practitioners have yet to come to agreement with regard to what is meant by many of the terms and expressions related to cyberspace. This is characteristic of any new field that serves broadly disparate populations. It is also extremely problematic when trying to come to grips with effective policy approaches for, describe requirements and objectives of, or conduct research about the domain.

In their new work, "Glossary of Cyber Warfare, Cyber Crime, Cyber Security," Dan Remenyi and Richard Wilson provide a great service to the field. Their glossary offers a starting point towards reaching consensus on the meanings and relevance of these terms. Not all will agree with all of their interpretations. Nonetheless, by putting their definitions in writing, they establish a solid point of departure for refinement.

Cyberspace is, after all, about effectively transmitting information. Agreed upon definitions for that information are at the root of effectively discussing and moving forward in this domain. This work moves us forward.

RADM (Ret) Janice M. Hamby, USN
Chancellor
NDU College of Information and Cyberspace
Fort Lesley J. McNair
Washington, DC, USA

iii

Preface

There has always been some degree of controversy surrounding computers and computers have always been vulnerable. In the early days of computing there were cases of theft and criminal damage to new computer installations. Computers have been shot at and even bombed, causing extensive damage.

Over the years there have been many attempts at computer fraud. One of the most celebrated was the so-called Salami Fraud where small amounts of money, which would be hardly noticed by any individual, were taken from a very large number of bank accounts, thus enriching the fraudsters. However, these were largely limited to corporate situations where the damage was contained. With the arrival of the personal computer and especially mobile devices such as laptops and smart phones the damage achievable by fraudsters and vandals and others wishing to inflict damage on elements of cyberspace has grown and a considerable number of people have had a lot of money swindled from them. In a similar vein computers are now also used as weapons to target other computers and electronic devices.

The past 20 years has seen a massive escalation in the damage done in cyberspace and this has been accompanied by a growing concern about all aspects of Cyber Security. The ever increasing number of cyber attacks on individuals, organisations and national government agencies has reached epidemic proportions. It is not possible to know the exact extent of these attacks and the damage which they have done as no one wishes to advertise their vulnerability - even their past vulnerability. However, estimates suggest that the cost of these attacks have run into tens or even hundreds of billions of dollars. What is certain is that billions of dollars are being spent every year in order to improve cyber security.

To support cyber professionals in their fight against cyber attacks the academic community has taken the subject to heart and there is today an extensive programme of academic research on many different aspects of the topic. It is a relatively new subject for university research and it comes with the need to acquire new vocabulary to describe the concepts and ideas which require the attention of the academic researcher. New words and expressions are always a challenge and it is for this reason that this glossary has been developed.

Two major areas of investigation that need to be explored by those interested in Cyber Security are cyber crime and cyber warfare. Both of these sets of activities are defended against by similar types of cyber security activities and thus an understanding of one will inevitably lead to an comprehension of the other.

Cybercrime refers to an illegal act which is perpetrated through the use of a computer either on a stand-alone basis or in network with other computer systems. There are many types of computer crimes, all of which involve the harming or compromising of an individual, an organization or a nation state. In order for an act to be regarded as a crime it is necessary for it to violate a law. Laws regarding what constitutes appropriate actions on computers vary considerably from country to country and therefore what is a cybercrime in one country might not be necessarily considered so in another country. Furthermore, there is the issue of jurisdiction, whereby the effect of the crime may be felt in a different area or country to where the act was initiated. Technically if an act is not punishable by criminal law it cannot be considered to be a crime.

The notion of cyber warfare is more difficult. Although this term is used in the media regularly it is contested in the sense that it has been argued that cyber warfare can only occur after a cyber war has been declared or if the cyber warfare antagonist's actions have been clearly identified and owned. Furthermore, the term warfare implies that a nation state or their direct agents are involved with the attack. To date no cyber war has been declared. However, what is more generally considered to be cyber warfare does occur and occurs too frequently without any declaration of war.

What is especially interesting about cyber security is that the topic is evolving and evolving quickly. Therefore, new concepts and ideas are continuing to be developed and all of these require explanation. In addition, while writing this Glossary it became clear just how broad the topic is. Cyber warfare, cyber crime, and cyber security embrace issues ranging from political science, to management and administration, to computer and data communications technology, and one of the great challenges has been to provide enough information for a competent definition without overloading the situation.

This first edition of the glossary addresses more than 500 definitions. A substantial bibliography is attached to the list of definitions and a supplementary list of web-based links to relevant websites is available to readers.

Dan Remenyi PhD

dan.remenyi@gmail.com

How to use this book

As with all glossaries and dictionaries this book has been designed to be dipped into at any point.

Readers will notice that the length of the definitions vary considerably. One of the objectives of the authors was to avoid too extensive definitions. When it comes to fairly technical issues this has been achieved. But on some of the more sociological issues, especially those related to political science and to management the definitions are somewhat longer.

A substantial bibliography has been provided, but we are aware that many readers will want to be able to use the Web in order to find supporting information. Some of the Websites we have made reference to have long URLs and it was decided not to include them in the paper copy of the book.

As a result, we have created an electronic copy of the URLs and this is available to any purchaser of the book by completing a short identification form from the following link.

http://academic-conferences.org/academic-publishing/cyber-links

It is hoped that readers will find this list of URLs useful. The links were tested during May 2018 and were active at this time.

Acknowledgments

The idea of producing this book occurred during the International Conference on Cyber Warfare and Security held in Washington in 2018 where it became apparent there was a need to reflect on the possible meaning of all the new ideas and concepts which were being incorporated in this field of study.

As a first step in producing this book, participants at the conference were invited to suggest concepts which should be included in the list of definitions. In all some hundred suggestions were received and the authors would like to thank those who responded to the call for suggestions.

About the authors

Dan Remenyi was first employed in the computer industry in 1965 when computers had little more to offer than their ability to perform high speed arithmetic. Over the years he made several attempts to escape from the cyber domain but has always found himself returning to this fascinating world. For the past 30 years he shared his attention between the academic side of ICT management and the consulting world and during this time cyber security has always been an important issue. However, today cyber security has moved to centre stage with the increase in cyber crime and now cyber warfare. Dan Remenyi has held Visiting Professorships at 10 different universities in four countries, including the United Kingdom, Ireland, Sweden and South Africa where he has both taught and researched. He lives and works in South Oxfordshire in the United Kingdom. He holds a BSocSc, MBA and a PhD.

Richard L. Wilson is currently a Professor in the Philosophy and Computer and Information Sciences Department at Towson University in Towson, Maryland. Professor Wilson is a specialist in Applied Ethics with over 30 years of teaching experience and a background that includes designing Engineering and Computer Science Ethics courses, as well as Business, Medical, and Environmental ethics courses. Richard Wilson is currently working in the areas of Cyber Warfare, Cyber Security, Cyber Espionage, and Cyber Crime. Areas of particular interest are Cyber and Bio Terrorism. Among his publications are articles highlighting the ethical issues related to Drones and UAV's, Hacking in the 2016 American Election, 3D Printing and Anticipatory Business Ethics, Fracking and anticipated ethical issues with CRISPR, gene editing technology. Richard Wilson was educated at Duquesne University in Pittsburgh, Pennsylvania.

Access control to Avatar

Term	Definition
Access control	When computers were large devices they were housed in a secure area with restrictions on who could enter the Computer Room. As computers reduced in size they spread throughout the organization. Although this allowed more people access to the devices it became necessary to restrict access to the data and the programs on the computers. As a result, access control was implemented through identification codes and passwords. More recently biometrics are used in addition or as an alternative to identification codes and passwords.
Act of war	Action normally undertaken by a hostile nation state against another nation state with whom it regards itself to be in active conflict i.e. at war. The initial act of war might be covert which then leads to outright kinetic hostilities.
	However, as can be seen by examining the entry on war in this glossary the term is used to describe a number of other states of conflict besides that of traditional warfare.
	See War.
Active cyber defense	This is a critically important but not well defined concept in cyber security. It involves the recognition of the vulnerability of computers and networks to cyber attacks from all possible

Term	Definition
	sources both external and internal. Active cyber defense requires a clearly articulated policy which will include issues related to how to identify threats, how to minimize the risk of an attack and how to ensure business (in its broadest sense) continuity in the event of such an attack taking place.
	Active cyber defense is a time-consuming and costly exercise and is not often executed with as much care and attention as it actually deserves.
Activist	A person who usually has strongly held beliefs and who is prepared to take action, normally in the form of campaigning, in order to bring about some change in society or the status quo in the world as a whole.
Advanced Persistent Threat (APT)	A threat to a computer network whereby an unauthorized individual gains access to a system and retains this capability for an extended period of time. The object of an advanced persistent threat is not normally to harm or damage a computer system or the network but rather the collection of data which has not been authorized by the owners of the system.
Adversary	A term used to describe any opponent. In the cyber warfare community, it would be usual to associate it with a high degree of malignant intent. An adversary could be potential or actual. An adversary could be external or internal, i.e. a member of the staff or an outsider.
	In cyberspace hackers and other individuals or entities who produce and distribute malware are the primary adversaries, although there are a number of others.

Term	Definition
Adversary behavior	In the context of cyberspace adversary behavior is represented by actions which are designed to do harm or at least compromise a computer system or network. This can range from theft of data to infecting the computer system with malware. It can be the product of simple vandalism or it can be executed with the intention of defrauding the owners of the computer or network. It can involve denial of service attacks or the destruction of data or software etc.
Agent based modeling	The activity of designing simulation activities to explore the interaction of autonomous agents in the form of either individuals or organizations with the view of assessing the effects of their behavior on a system as a whole. The purpose of this may be training or attempting to find vulnerabilities in the system.
Air gapping	To air gap a system means to isolate the system from local area networks or public WiFi networks. Air gapping is a security measure that is aimed at protecting a system from intrusion. Air gapping delivers a high degree of security, but it significantly reduces functionality.
Alt right, The	The AltRight or alternative right is a term used to describe a rather vaguely defined group of individuals or organizations on the far right ring of the political spectrum. They are generally considered to be beyond conservative and have entered an area of extremism.
Alternative media	What is identified as alternative media often depends on the point of view of the speaker. The term alternative media usually refers to news sources which someone is not accustomed with using. Thus to the political establishment

Term	Definition
	in the USA the alternative media would be almost any media outlet other than the Washington Post and the New York Times, The Wall Street Journal as well as NBC, Fox and CNN. Alternative media would include news obtained from Twitter, Facebook and a variety of Web based news providers.
American legal system	The system of laws, functions and institutions which govern civil life in the USA. It is administered through the justice system which includes the police, courts and other agencies. The American legal system is based on both the Constitution, statuary laws, administrative regulations and on concepts of Common Law. Common Law means that cases which are heard in the courts effectively become part of the law as the law relies on precedents which affect future judgments in the courts.
Analytic Hierarchy Process (AHP)	A structured technique for organizing and analyzing complex decisions. It is especially relevant to group decision making.
Analytic Network Process (ANP)	A more general form of the analytic hierarchy process (AHP) used in multi-criteria decision analysis. ANP structures a decision problem into a network. Both ANP and AHP use a system of pairwise comparisons to measure the weights of the components of the structure, and finally to rank the alternatives in the decision.
Anonymity	In cyberspace anonymity occurs when the originator of a message, an email or a website is not displayed and therefore his or her identity is unknown. It is intended to allow individuals to freely express themselves without any direct or indirect consequence, but this is not necessarily

Term	Definition
	the case. It has become increasingly difficult for anonymity to be achieved within cyberspace although advocates of the Dark Web enthusiastically argue that one of the main advantages of this specific aspect of cyberspace is that it allows them to retain at least some degree of anonymity. Web browsers such as TOR allow Internet users to retain their anonymity.
Anonymous	Anonymous is the name given to a decentralized group of hackers who have a political agenda which represents general resentment against the current social, economic and political systems in the Western world. Anonymous has been active since 2003. Their activities have been described as hacktivist. Their supporters see them as digital freedom fighters (fighting against big corporations and big governments) while their adversaries regard them as cyber terrorists. They are known for their activities with respect to denial of service attacks.
Anti Forensics	Anti Forensics techniques hide information concerning a cyber attack and/or create false trails implicating innocent parties. Anti forensics consists of techniques which can make the attribution of any given cyber attack quite difficult.
Anti spyware	This is an antidote to spyware. Software which detects the presence and neutralizes the effect of spyware. There is now a wide range of antispyware products available on the market. *See Spyware.*
Antivirus Software	A program or set of programs which will detect and prevent viruses from contaminating a computer system or a network. It is now regarded as

Term	Definition
	essential that every computer system which is connected to the Internet should be protected using antivirus software. Antivirus software needs to be continually updated to counter new malware which is continually being updated and developed by attackers.
Arab spring	The Arab Spring (also known as the Arab revolutions) began on 18 December 2010 in Tunisia. The Arab Spring was a revolutionary wave of demonstrations, both violent and non violent in nature, and which brought forth civil wars in North Africa as well as the Middle East. The Revolution spread to five other countries: Libya, Egypt, Yemen, Syria and Bahrain, where regimes were toppled and nations faced anti government protests.
	It has been asserted that social software made a significant contribution to the ability of the protesters to confront government forces during the various demonstrations which took place.
Arms race	The struggle between malicious hackers and the authorities who are working to defend computers and networks against malicious attacks has been referred to as an arms race. New approaches to the development of malware and new processes for the defrauding of individuals are continually being developed. In order to prevent harm from these activities organizations and governments are continually developing new strategies to fight the criminals involved.
	The term arms race likens these cyber activities to those of nation states which try to acquire larger and more destructive weapons in order to

Term	Definition
	outdo their potential or real opponents.
Art of War	Ancient Chinese text on how to pursue war by a highly respected military philosopher Sun-Tzu. Written in the BCE era it is still today regarded as an important text appertaining to the conducting of warfare.
	The Art of War is in fact regarded as an all-time classic and the principles on which its teachings are based have been used in both the military and business worlds.
Artificial Intelligence (AI)	Computer software developed to imitate one or more intellectual characteristics of the human mind. The original concept was that artificial intelligence would be able to match human intelligence. However, in recent years any introduction of decision-making within the electronics of devices has been referred to as artificial intelligence.
	An early proponent of the concept of artificial intelligence, Alan Turing, suggested that it would be achieved when, in conversation with a computer, it was not possible for a human to be able to say with certainty that the entity with whom the conversation was being held was or was not a human.
	Machine learning and neural networks have advanced the level of intelligence which is available in smart machines. However, the ultimate aim of creating a device which resembles human mental capacity is still far away.
Assange, Julian	Julian Assange is a computer programmer and editor of well-known WikiLeaks. WikiLeaks was drawn to international attention after a se-

Term	Definition
	ries of leaks provided information on USA military actions and failures. Some of the information the leaks revealed were occasions of friendly fire in Bagdad and information on the deaths of civilians. Although the charges of rape have been dropped he currently faces prosecution for the leaks and he currently resides in the Ecuadorian Embassy in London as a result of these warrants and is unable to leave that building without facing arrest.
Attack signature or digital trace	All computer activity or transactions can be identified by codes created by the cyber devices used to initiate the attack or to transmit it through a network. In cyber warfare these codes are sometimes referred to attack signatures or are also known as digital traces. With enough guile it is possible to disguise an attack signature or make it so complicated that it is difficult to identity.
Attack surface	This is the sum of the different points or opportunities which an attacker can use to damage or harm a computer or network system. Each point on the attack surface is a potential target. There are often a large number of such targets. It is important to understand the attack surface as it maps out the potential areas of risk.
Attack vector	A path or means by which an attacker can gain access to a computer to introduce malware or some other form of harm to the target. The attack vector is the trajectory along which the aim is taken at the target system.
Attacks against individuals	Hostile actions which are focused towards one or more individual or person as opposed to organizations. One of the most frequent types of

Term	Definition
	this attack is so called phishing, whereby a fraudster tries to obtain personal information about the target so that an identity theft can take place. Another well known type of attack is when the fraudster pretends to be an employee of. e. g., Microsoft and they call the target to say that there is a fault or potential fault with his or her computer demanding a fee has to be paid in order to rectify the situation.
Attacks against nation states	Hostile actions which are aimed at a whole country or a large section of it. This could be in the form of an attack against critical infrastructure or it could be an assault on Government Departments. Attacks against individuals (except if the individual was a prominent politician) or non-governmental organizations would not usually be considered an attack against a National State.
Attacks against websites	Hostile actions which are aimed at interrupting or destroying a website or a group of websites. There are a large variety of ways in which these attacks can take place and the results of these attacks may be quite different. Sometimes the website is vandalized and sometimes the links on the website are replaced taking anyone who uses the website to pornographic images. On other occasions attacks against websites are used to obtain personal information about users of the website to attempt fraud.
Attribution	In the cyberspace context attribution normally refers to the naming of a source of an attack. Sometimes attribution is obvious as in the case of ransom ware where the criminal attackers are seeking a payment from the target. At other

Term	Definition
	times it can be quite difficult to be certain to whom to attribute a cyber attack.
Audit trail	A security-relevant chronological list that provides documentary evidence of the sequence of activities that have affected a specific operation.
Autonomous Micro UAVs	A military device similar to a drone which comprises a miniaturized flying robot which can navigate in difficult areas. These small miniature devices are intended to be used in groups referred to as swarms. *See UAV and UAS.*
Avatar	A digital representation of a person, animal or figure used to represent a person online. It may be used in one application or across various platforms i.e. in a video game, or an Internet forum. Avatars are a key feature of the program Second Life which is a comprehensive life simulation used for both entertainment and learning.

B

Backlash to Bugs Bounty

Term	Definition
Backlash	A negative reaction to any action which leads to an adverse situation for the perpetrator of the original action. The problem which a backlash presents is that it can be so severe that it does more than counter whatever objectives that were set for the original action. The extent and severity of a backlash can be a surprise.
Backup	The creation of copies of software and data which is stored remotely and which can be used to reinstate a computer system after it has been damaged by a cyber attack.
Big data	Large scale databases used for data mining techniques. The objective of this type of computing is to look for relationships between variables in the extra large databases for the purposes of enquiry or research. The use of the term big data was first employed in the 1990s as a result of faster and more efficient hardware and software. The size of the datasets used in big data applications generally go beyond the ability of commonly used software products and may involve terabytes or even petabytes of data.
Big data policing	Because Big Data is relatively new and not yet used by large numbers of organizations, it is not yet clear how influential big data is or will be in society. Some argue that special controls are needed to police big data sets. The Cambridge

Term	Definition
	Analytica controversy and the revelation that Facebook gave access to the records of approximately 70 million of its users suggest that big data needs to be carefully controlled. How this could be accomplished is not yet clear. Big Data is also used by police solve crimes.
Biometrics	In cyberspace biometrics is the use of unique and identifiable bodily characteristics in order to identify individuals. Thus biometrics consists of fingerprints, iris impressions, hand geometry, voice recognition etc. It has been suggested that it is the most reliable way of identifying and individual. Biometrics is increasingly considered to be a useful way to ensure the secure access of an individual to his or her computer and network.
Bit nation	A voluntary society of individuals who wish to identify themselves as citizens of the Internet. Created in 2014 by a Swiss based individual it is a voluntary group which is now believed to exceed 2000 and is associated with Bitcoin. It is not entirely clear what its objects really mean and to what extent they could be achieved.
Bitcoin	A digital currency with no physical denominations which resides online. Bitcoin is decentralized and uses peer-to-peer payment networks. Although shares in the organization promoting Bitcoin have been successful with its value soaring in the past few years, this value is considered to be unstable. As Bitcoin is not based on a national currency there is concern that it will bypass the national regulations governing the issue and use of monetary instruments.

Term	Definition
Black hat	The term used to describe a hacker who is intent on causing harm to a computer or network system. It is a reference to old fashioned cowboy films where the "bad" guys tended to wear black hats.
Black market	The market for goods and services which are not regarded as part of legitimate commerce. In the context of cyberspace black market commodities available through the Dark Web include narcotic drugs, human body parts, weapons and other illegal products or services. The extent to which the Dark Web represents a black market is unknown to the authors, however it is the contention of the media that almost every commodity and service imaginable can be purchased there.
Black ops	A popular video game. The term Black Ops is also used to describe a covert operation arranged by a government agency or a military authority. The word "Black" is sometimes used as a generic term for any hidden or secret activity.
Blackhat USA	Conference held in the USA and abroad which attracts a wide audience of those interested in cyber security. It has two streams, one of which consists of cyber briefings and the other cyber training.
Blackout day	A social media event created to encourage the posting of content that is made by and features everyday black people. Typically takes place on Tumblr, Facebook and Twitter, Blackout Day is considered a form of creative digital activism.

Term	Definition
Blended ops	The idea behind Blended Ops is that a target is attacked in more than one way. One suggested strategy or tactic for a Blended Ops is to recruit someone in the organization being attacked. This would make a powerful combination but such an attack would require a considerable amount of time, close attention and expense.
Blockchain	A blockchain is an arrangement of data records in a continuous growing list which has been designed to assure a maximum level of security. The records are distributed across the web and thus this method of storage of records is regarded as being highly resistant to modification. It is typically used as a ledger in peer-to-peer transactions.
Blue team	In simulation exercises designed to test cyber resilience the team of individuals who are defending against an attack on the computer system or network are often referred to as the *blue team*.
Bot	A short form of the word robot which in cyberspace is a program which travel across the web and can simulate the presence of a human actor. This type of program often collects data from the web such as e-mail addresses.
Botnets	A number of computers or Internet-connected devices, each of which is running one or more bots. Botnets can be used to distributed denial-of-service attacks, steal data, and allow access to devices and their connections. *See Zombie Bots.*

Term	Definition
Bugs bounty	It is notoriously difficult to remove all bugs from software products and thus there are often problems with early versions of software. A bugs bounty is a program offered by a number of software developers to individuals who are prepared to test their software in order to locate problems or flaws in the system. A payment is made to these individuals who contribute to the processes of improving the software product they have been testing.

C

4Chan to Cyberspace superiority

Term	Definition
4Chan	An English language imageboard website based in Japan which has been linked to cyber misconduct of various sorts. It has been functioning since 2003. An imageboard is an Internet forum which operates mostly with pictures and images.
Cambridge Analytica	A privately owned business which is involved in psychographic targeting on a global scale affecting election management. It has come under heavy criticism for its involvement in the Brexit referendum in the United Kingdom and in the last presidential election in the USA of America.
Camera blocker	Some mobile computer users worry that the camera on their devices may be switched on remotely in order to spy on them. A camera blocker is device which is placed over the built in camera in a mobile computer which prevents spy software from being used to observe the user of the computer.
CAP attacks	CAP stands for Card Authentication Protocol which drives and controls the connection between remote point-of-sale devices and ATMs and the computers behind them.
Cashing it out	In the cyberspace environment, "cashing it out" refers to the processing or converting fraudulent transactions into actual cash. This is often done

Term	Definition
	by using stolen credit card details to purchase some items which can then be exchanged for cash. An example of this is buying gift vouchers with a stolen credit card which can be subsequently refunded in some way for actual money.
Catastrophic attack	An attack which causes substantial damage and from which there is considerable difficulty recovering. What will be regarded as catastrophic will vary from one person to another and from one organization to another. In one environment a computer or network failure for a few minutes could cause catastrophic harm and in another a computer or network could be unserviceable for day without causing catastrophic harm. The more attention that is given to security issues the less likely an organization will suffer a catastrophic attack and feel its consequences.
Chaos Computer Conference (CCC)	A conference held by Europe's largest association of hackers. Based in Germany the Chaos Computer Club traces its roots back to the 1980s when hacking was not seen in quite the negative light with which it is perceived today. CCC defines itself in the following way, *"a galactic community of life forms, independent of age, sex, race or society orientation, which strives across borders for freedom of information."*
Chat bot	A program on the Internet with which a person can conduct a limited conversation (audio or textual) as though it were a human. Some chat bots can be tailor made to engage in particular types of conversations.

Term	Definition
Child pornography	Regarded by some as a form of pedophilia, child pornography is an illegal form of pornography in a number of different parts of the world. It shows either still pictures or videos of children being sexually abused. This crime is actively pursued by law enforcement agencies as it is held that there is a connection between child pornography and pedophilia.
Closed network	A collection of computers and other cyber assets which are connected with limiting access. They are not connected to the Internet. Intranets are closed systems.
Cloud computing	The practice of using a network of remote computers hosted in a variety of different locations on the Internet for the purposes of storing, processing and distributing data and information. Cloud computing needs to be contrasted with a different approach whereby computers were generally connected to a relatively local server or host. Cloud computing is a relatively recent development which takes advantage of the ubiquitous of Internet connectivity. However, it has the problem that it is not necessarily clear where all the data of an organization is actually stored and backed up on the planet and this can give rise to a number of concerns.
Collateral damage	A cyber attack can cause damage to other individuals, organizations and cyber systems in addition to the intended target. The other individuals, organizations, or cyber systems harmed, are referred to as collateral damage. Collateral damage is always a substantial concern in any conflict and in general, combatants normally at-

Term	Definition
	tempt to minimize this. However sometimes it is not possible and innocent bystanders are hurt by a struggle which is of no direct concern to them.
Collateral murder video	A classified USA video released by Wikileaks in 2007 showing the attack by a USA Apache helicopter on civilians in Baghdad. The USA Government expressed displeasure at the release of this video. It later transpired that a American Army intelligence analyst released the video and was arrested and charged and sentenced to 35 years' imprisonment.
Combatant	An entity, a person or a nation state, with which one is at war or at least in a state of active hostility. In cyberspace it is not always clear who the combatants are as much of the action tends to be covert.
Command and control warfare	The activities of an event being planned or masterminded centrally. It also means that any changes have to be authorized by an individual or the group which is in control of the event.
Common criteria certified	The Common Criteria for Information Technology Security Evaluation is an international standard for computer security certification. It dates back to the 1990s and was established by collaboration between France, Germany, the Netherlands and the UK. With reference to these standards producers of cyber devices can make claims about their attributes and these can be tested and verified.
Communication threats	The term communication threat has a number of different possible meanings. A communication threat could constitute an attempt to disrupt the data communication facilities associated with a

Term	Definition
	computer or network. It could also be an attack on an organization's email facilities. At a different level the term could have a more personal meaning in that it relates to the behavior of individuals and how it affects others. A wide range of threats may be made across the Internet and one of these in particular concerns computer or cyber bullying which mostly affects young people and has in a number of recent cases led to juvenile suicide.
	Although not necessarily illegal cyber bullying is considered to be an abhorrent practice which needs to be controlled and for which there is currently not adequate education available.
Competitor	An entity, a person, an organization or a nation state, with which one is in a state of rivalry or contention. Competition may be friendly or it may be hostile. In the commercial world competition is often regarded as a healthy state of affairs, but it can also be a precursor to conflict.
Comprehensive National Cybersecurity Initiative (CNCI)	The CNCI was the result of the enactment of National Security Directive 54/Homeland Security Presidential Directive 23 (NSPD-54/HSPD-23) in January 2008. This initiative was enacted by George W. Bush. It addresses USA cyber security goals and spans multiple agencies including the Department of Homeland Security, the Office of Management and Budget, and the National Security Agency.
Computer based personality judgments	Software that assess personality traits of computer users. This software predicts the likely behavior of individuals based on their social software exchanges especially the indications given by Likes and Dislikes icons. This type of

Term	Definition
	software has been used for marketing purposes but recently it has been revealed that it was also employed in elections in order to help political parties target individuals who are likely to be sympathetic to their policies. The Cambridge Analytica controversy is based on the use of such software.
Computer fraud	A wide ranging term which describes many different activities related to the misrepresentation of situations in order to take inappropriate advantage of an individual or an organization. The result of a fraud is normally the acquisition of an illegal financial advantage by the fraudster. Computer fraud can involve the misrepresentation of a number of different types of business transactions including the changing of computer records in order to indicate a payment has been made when in fact it was not. It could also involve inappropriate transfers of funds from one account to another. These would be internal acts of computer fraud. Other activities which could be described as computer fraud include those where criminals contact individual computer users and attempt to extort money from them on the grounds that they can prevent their computers from encountering a variety of different types of problems. This has sometimes been referred to as the MicroSoft scam as the fraudsters tend pretends to be employed by that company. Cybercrime related to issues such as phishing and ransom activities could also be described as computer fraud.

Term	Definition
Computer intrusion	When an outsider penetrates or accesses a computer or network when he or she has no authority to so do. A computer intrusion may not result in any harm to any of the cyber assets involved.
Computer intrusion detection	Methods by which any attempt to gain access to a computer system are identified and perhaps prevented.
Computer misuse	This is a general term describing the use of a computer in some way other than what it was intended to be used for. Computer misuse ranges from an employee using his or her employer's machine for personal email to initiating a cyber attack through his or her own machine.
Computer Network Attack (CNA)	An attempt to either destroy or damage an organization's computer network. This is a high level attack which will cause damage to a significant number of cyber assets. Such an attack would cause serious disruption to the working of an organization.
Computer Network Defense (CND)	As network attacks are potentially so damaging organizations will generally devote considerable time and resources to diminishing the possibility of such an attack and will do whatever is necessary in order to quickly recover. A computer network defense represents the actions required to avoid computer network attack and to minimize the effect of any attack.
Computer Network Exploitation (CNE)	The means by which a system can be used to infiltrate a target computer network in order to identify and gather intelligence data. It involves using a computer network in a hostile manner in order to gain the advantage of surreptitiously acquiring unauthorized data.

Term	Definition
Confirmation bias	The tendency for researchers to find data or to interpret data in a way which supports their original opinion. It is recognized as a major concern for any researcher but especially those engaged in academic research.
Conspiracism	The belief that dark nefarious forces are behind events ranging from the assassination of JFK to the attack on the Twin Towers on 9/11. There are those who believe that NASA did not send men to the moon. Those who tend to believe in complex plots behind what are probably simple circumstances are regarded as conspiracy theorists. Conspiracy theories are often quite implausible and relatively easy to disregard.
Content industry	For the Internet to be useful, it has to contain a variety of different forms of data on a wide variety of subjects, and when discussing this in terms of cyberspace, these types of data are often referred to as content. The content industry is all the players who produce content in either text or music or video form. The content industry is a large market with many thousands of players from all around the world.
Convention on Cybercrime	The Convention on Cybercrime also known as the Budapest Convention on Cybercrime was adopted by the Committee of Ministers of the Council of Europe on 8 November 2004. Its principal objective is to establish a common criminal policy aimed at the protection of society against cybercrime.
Copyright	Protection provided by law to individuals or organizations that have created or written work and preventing it from being copied and used by others without explicit permission from the

Term	Definition
	originator of the work. Many countries have copyright laws but there are numerous countries which do not. Copyright is protected in each country for a specific period of time which ranges from about one hundred years to only a few years. If copyright is breached, then the offended party is in a position to take legal action against individuals or organizations that have illegitimately used the material which was protected by the copyright. However for such action to be affective it may be necessary for the offender to be resident in a country which has appropriate copyright laws.
Cost of cyber security	It has been estimated that in 2017 the global cost of cyber attacks was more than $120 Billion. It is not possible to verify the accuracy of this figure.
Counter intelligence	The work undertaken to collect and analyze data for the purpose of illuminating or reducing the possibility that espionage activity or an act of sabotage will be committed against the state.
Courage foundation	A trust founded in 2013, created for fundraising to pay the legal defense of individuals such as whistleblowers and journalists. They claim "We defend Snowden, Hammond, Brown and other truth tellers"
Covert act	An attack which is carried out in a surreptitious way so that the source of the attack is unknown. The Cold War between the USA and its allies and the Soviet Union was conducted mostly through covert acts.
Cozy Bear	A group of advanced Russian hackers who are believed to be state sponsored. They appeared to

Term	Definition
	favor the Clinton Presidential campaign over the Bernie Saunders' campaign. It is one of a pair of such groups of hackers; the other one is referred to as Fancy Bear.
Creative Commons	A not-for-profit initiative supported by a range of organizations and individuals devoted to allowing creative work to be held in the public domain and used and built upon and shared. It is the opposite of copyright material.
Creative defense	A creative defense is the opposite of a reactive cyber security as it anticipates cyber attacks, and uses techniques such as honey tokens to deflect attacks.
Crest	A not-for-profit organization which describes itself as "assurance in information security". It is a trade organization which supplies technical information to the market place interested in issues related to assurance in information security.
Crime scripting	An activity which helps to understand the nature of a crime. It effectively deconstructs criminal events into their component parts for the purposes of developing a set of outcome focused recommendations. Crime scripting is an effective framework for collating and consolidating data in order to establish a sequence of decisions and actions within a particular crime context.
Crimeware	Any hardware, software or firmware which has been developed for the purposes of engaging in criminal activities. Pirated software or fake hardware would not generally be considered as crimeware.

Term	Definition
Critical information infrastructure	The devices, systems, legislation and individuals which are necessary to allow cyberspace to function in the way in which it is intended. The critical information infrastructure can also be seen as the culture which promotes and sustains interest in the growth of cyberspace.
Cross site scraping	A form of Web Scraping involving a number of websites. *See Web scraping.*
Crowd sourcing	The pledging and sometimes the collection of money (or other resources) from individuals who have been canvassed for contributions over the Internet. Crowdsourcing often involves a large number of small amounts of money which aggregate to a large amount of funds. It has been used particularly successfully to launch new organizations. Crowdsourcing has been used in both the commercial and the charity sectors were large sums of money have been required. It is regarded by many as being a leveling activity which allows small enterprises or activities to compete with larger organizations or events.
Crypto anarchist	An individual who proposes that the Internet should be unregulated with strong emphasis on the use of anonymity. Crypto anarchists are part of a larger movement of cyber anarchists who argue that it is unnecessary to construct any regulatory framework for the operation of cyberspace and that all the actors in this arena should be allowed to behave in any way they wish. Crypto anarchists represent an extreme form of

Term	Definition
	a laissez-faire attitude to the development, growth and application of cyber assets, both hardware and software. There is a Crypto Anarchist Manifesto. Although there is no great appetite for centralized control of cyberspace neither is there approval of the views expressed by crypto anarchists.
Crypto currency	A form of digital money which lies outside of the normal monetary controls, designed to be secure and anonymous and monitored and controlled by nation states. Bitcoin is an example of a crypto currency and a number of central banks have expressed their concern about the stability of this type of currency as a monetary instrument. Bunny Coin which was designed to facilitate adult purchases is another example of a crypto currency.
Cyber	Appertaining to the use or involvement of information and communications technology (ICT). The word Cyber is used in a number of different situations which can be seen from the many entries below in this glossary.
Cyber abuse	Cyber Abuse is any online behavior which is reasonably likely to cause offence. Cyber bulling and trolling are typical acts of cyber abuse. However, there are several other forms including hate email and stalking to mention only two.
Cyber activism	The tendency of certain groups to play an active and easily recognizable role in molding current opinion with regards to cyberspace. There are cyber activists who are enthusiastic about the current trends in cyberspace and who advocate a

Term	Definition
	laissez-faire attitude in the belief that this will facilitate the delivery of more benefits to individuals, to organizations and to society as a whole. At the same time there are cyber activists who oppose this position and believe that it is imperative that cyberspace be closely monitored and controlled by governmental authorities. *See e-Activism.*
Cyber anarchy	The suggestion that there is no form of control in cyberspace and that any of the players are at liberty to undertake any course of action they desire. Although cyberspace is not "heavily" regulated there are a number of norms which ensure that the behavior of the major players do not fall outside accepted limits. These largely informal norms provide a limited amount of guidance but are not regarded as adequate by certain players in cyberspace. Those who propose cyber anarchy claim that any control on cyberspace limits creativity and therefore impacts everyone.
Cyber asset	Any computer or network device either in the form of hardware, firmware or software which enables an organization's or individual's access to and use of cyberspace, may be regarded as a cyber asset.
Cyber attack	A hostile act initiated through a computer or a computer network system, which is intended to harm an individual, organization or nation state directly or indirectly. A cyber attack may be as simple as an attempt to infect a computer with a virus, or it may be as complicated as an attempt to destroy a complete computer system. Cyber attacks may be committed for malicious reasons

Term	Definition
	only, or they may be part of the greater plan which could range from extortion to attempting to interfere with future plans of the entity which is under attack. By their nature cyber attacks are generally low cost, high speed and sometimes difficulty to attribute.
Cyber attack retaliation/ response	A cyber attack which is conducted by an entity after an attack had been initiated against it. This could be described as a tit-for-tat response.
Cyber black-mail	A form of cyber coercion or extortion which may involve compromising sexual photographs or other material which embarrasses the target of the attack. It shares many of the characteristics of cyber ransom.
Cyber bullying	A wide ranging concept which normally refers to the use of cyber devices to harass individuals with abusive messages. In cyberspace this is usually unwanted and unpleasant commentary, name calling, unfounded accusations and threats of various sorts. Cyber bullying is perhaps of greatest concern among children and students especially those at primary and secondary school, where it has been found to have caused considerable harm to individuals. However, cyber bullying also exists in the adult world and there are many examples of politicians and other highly visible members of our society being showered with abusive emails. Women report much higher levels of such abuse than men.
Cyber coercion	Cyber coercion could be seen as a result of steps taken by the authorities to ensure that cyberspace is not chaotic, but this term could also be used to describe attacks made by individuals or organizations to compel different types of action

Term	Definition
	to be taken. The Sony Pictures Entertainment cyber attack has been described as a coercion attack. In a sense blackmail is a form of coercion and vice versa.
Cyber command (CYCOM)	That part of a nation's military which has been tasked with ensuring that the cyber capability of a nation state adequate to face any contingency which might arise. Cyber command is often focused on ensuring that the nation's cyber defenses are state-of-the-art. In some cases cyber command may also look at offensive cyber strategies as well as defensive ones.
Cyber conflict	A general and wide-ranging term which can be used to describe any situation in which opponents attempt to use their cyber resources in competition with each other. Cyber conflict could be as simple as competitors attempting to develop the most sophisticated website in order to enhance its offering to the marketplace. It could also involve far more sinister acts in terms of one organization attempting to disrupt or sabotage the computer or network facilities of another.
Cyber crime	An illegal act which is perpetrated through the use of a computer either on a standalone basis or in network with other computer systems. There is a wide range of computer crimes all of which involve the harming or compromising of some individual or organization or nation state. In order for an act to be regarded as a crime it is necessary for it to violate a law. Laws regarding what are appropriate actions on computers vary considerably from country to country and therefore what is a cyber crime in one country might

Term	Definition
	not be necessarily considered so in another country. Furthermore, there is the issue of jurisdiction whereby the effect of the crime may be felt in an area or a country which may be different to where the act was initiated.
	Technically if an act is not punishable by criminal law it cannot be considered to be a crime.
Cyber culture	The group of people who are concerned with and work in the cyberspace environment tend to be of a particular type with relation to their skills, education, and sometimes their value sets. This applies not only to technical, but also to management and even academic individuals. In addition, cyberspace in most countries will have similar types of institutions and perhaps not dissimilar laws and regulations.
	Taking all these different human characteristics together it is possible to suggest that cyberspace has an individual and unique cyber culture which distinguishes it from the rest of society. This cyber culture is an evolving entity.
Cyber deception	Deception is about being dishonest and hiding motives or identity or other issues, which the perpetrator does not want known. Deception is the essence of a covert operation. Cyber attacks are often covert in order to prevent the identity of the culprit being known as this could lead to legal action or retaliation. In order to understand any given cyber attack it is necessary to understand the deception in order to try to prevent further attacks and do something about them.
Cyber Defense Management	An organization set up by NATO in Brussels in 2014 to offer a fast response to cyber attacks on

Term	Definition
Authority (CDMA)	members' critical national cyber infrastructures. It affirms the realization that cyberspace is another theatre of war.
Cyber Defense Structured Awareness (CDSA)	A book published by Springer laying out the key issues in cyber defense.
Cyber deterrence	The range of devices and systems and legislation which is available to attempt to prevent cyber crimes from taking place.
Cyber devices	The range of equipment which may be used to support individuals or organizations in their endeavors within cyberspace. The term cyber device would normally be synonymous with cyber asset.
Cyber disruption	This occurs when a computer or a network is unable to function in terms of its normal operational limitations. It could be the result of a direct attack, such as a denial of service attack, which could be described as cyber sabotage. A cyber disruption could last minutes, hours, days or even longer. A disruption attack will not normally cause any lasting damage to the cyber assets. It can be very damaging to an organization.
Cyber economy	This term could have at least two different meanings. The first could be a description of the wide range of elements in the market for cyber devices, hardware and software, and for the people necessary to ensure that cyberspace functions. A second meaning of the term cyber economy expresses how the physical economy has been

Term	Definition
	altered by the arrival of online services. Cyber developments have radically changed a number of aspects of retailing, government services, and health service delivery to mention only three of many aspects of our economy.
Cyber enabled economic warfare	Once again this term could have at least two different meanings. Economic warfare could refer to strong competitive interaction among actors in the market place and the competitive nature of many organizations within the marketplace, which have been sharpened by their employment of online systems. This is evident in retailing and air travel to mention only two industries. Cyber enabled economic warfare could also refer to attacks on institutions critical to the economy such as banks and other financial institutions in order to disrupt the normal functioning of the country.
Cyber environment	All the physical, cultural, legal, human, intellectual, emotional, and eco issues surrounding and interacting with cyber policy at the national level, organizational level and the personal level. The cyber environment continues to evolve at a rapid pace as new products and services are developed and new threats are created, requiring new ways of defending against these threats.
Cyber espionage	Espionage refers to activities related to spying on enemies or potential enemies. All forms of surreptitious data acquisition could be considered as cyber espionage provided it is collected with the intention acquiring an advantage, or perhaps desiring to do harm to an enemy or a potential enemy.

Term	Definition
Cyber event	A cyber event may be regarded as any incident which involves the use of a computer or network, which is worthy of being brought to the attention of management or the authorities. In the cyber security space such an event would relate to an attack or an attempted attack on the computer or network.
Cyber exploitation	The term exploitation can simply mean use, but in the cyberspace environment the term cyber exploitation is normally associated with some sort of cyber espionage, and involves the misuse of computers and networks by nefarious forces working against an individual, an organization or a government. *See cyber blackmail and cyber ransom.*
Cyber extortion	Extortion is a form of criminal activity whereby money is demanded from a target who is threatened with harm if the money is not paid. It can also be referred to as Demanding Money with Menaces. There are a number of ways in which this can be done one of which is described in the section on Ransom. *See cyber blackmail.*
Cyber forensics	The acquisition and preservation of evidence related to cyber matters in such a way that it will be acceptable in a court of law. Forensic science always refers to the careful inspection of evidence and the application or scientific principles.
Cyber fraud	A wide-ranging term which is used to describe the use of any cyber or ICT asset or device, hardware or software, to misrepresent a situation and thereby obtain illegally some ad-

Term	Definition
	vantage. Cyber fraud is an increasingly common form of cybercrime and it is often difficult to prosecute the perpetrators.
Cyber friend	The term cyber friend can be used in several different contexts. In the first place the term can be used to mean a contact which an individual makes with an entity through the Internet. The word friend is used in Facebook to mean someone who is apparently known to someone else. However, it is possible that the apparent friend could be someone entirely different to what he or she purports/pretends to be. It is also possible that the friend could be an organization rather than an individual. AI systems are now sufficiently sophisticated to be able to appear to be a human friend. Cyber friends can be initiators of scams such as the Romance scam. The words cyber friend could also be used to refer to a traditional friend who has moved away and with whom an individual remains in contact through email or some other social media platform.
Cyber grooming	Actions undertaken in order to prepare an individual to be involved in some activity. It is normally used in the context of befriending an individual and encouraging them to participate in some socially unacceptable behavior. The term is often associated is pedophilia.
Cyber infiltration	Cyber infiltration normally occurs when an actor uses a piece of malware to surreptitiously gain access to the target's computer or network system. The malware could remain dormant for a long period before being triggered by some event. The term cyber infiltration has also been

Term	Definition
	used to describe using the Internet to try to recruit jihadists in Western countries. *See Logic bomb.*
Cyber infrastructure	All the elements which are necessary and sufficient for cyberspace to function effectively. This ranges from the supply of electricity to the availability of components. It also includes having the right staff to operate sophisticated devices and to have in place, an appropriate range of legislation to ensure law and order within cyberspace.
Cyber insurgency	The term insurgency refers to an active revolt or an uprising against the authorities. It is possible to understand at least some of the antisocial if not criminal activities perpetrated through cybercrime as being part of a cyber insurgency. Some commentators would regard the group referred to as *Anonymous* as being a manifestation of cyber insurgency. *See Anonymous.*
Cyber intelligence	This term refers to the collecting of information across a wide spectrum of cyber activities. However, the word intelligence is used also to describe information in the military environment. Therefore, cyber intelligence is normally focused on attempting to discover who is likely to initiate cyber attacks and how these attacks might be conducted and what are the likely consequences of such attacks.
Cyber killchain	In terms of military targeting the notion of the cyber killchain is related to moving from intelligence gathering to the identification of appro-

Term	Definition
	priate targets, which in turn leads to the processes of engagement and perhaps destruction of an adversary or an adversary's cyber assets.
Cyber manipulation	The use of any form of cyber device to produce a result which would not occur otherwise, may be regarded as cyber manipulation. This can happen with both hardware and software and also with data. Criminals deploy cyber manipulation when they create fake frontages to ATM machines to swallow bank cards and capture PIN numbers. Security services have been alleged to influence firmware to obtain access to cyber assets and such behavior could be described as cyber manipulation.
Cyber native	A synonym for digital native, i.e. an individual who has been introduced to the word of cyber at an early age, and who has grown up with cyber and digital technology. *See Digital native.*
Cyber operations	The application of resources in a live situation. The term is used to describe the actualization of planned activities within cyberspace either from the point of view of normal computer and network operations or from the perspective of defending one's own cyber assets. Cyber operations could also involve counter offensive activities.
Cyber physical systems	A wide-ranging term which can be used to refer to the combination of hardware, firmware, software, infrastructural assets and people which constitute the components of an integrated cyber

Term	Definition
	system. The total amount of physical resources required to operate a cyber system is always much greater than the cyber devices themselves. The term can also be used to describe the technology required for cyber devices to be able to control situations involving manufacturing, aerospace, and chemical processes including the production of energy.
Cyber policy	In the early years of computers and networks they were simply seen as being tools of administration and were usually acquired without much consideration as to how they were to be properly used and how these assets were to be protected and controlled. This is no longer the case and all cyber assets are now more frequently believed to be important elements in and organizations strategy. For this reason, it has become essential for organizations to develop carefully articulated cyber policies which cover issues such as the acquisition of cyber assets, the employment of these assets, staffing issues, how the assets will be protected and what needs to be done in the event of cyber attacks. All of these issues should be addressed in an organizational cyber policy. *See Cyberspace operations.*
Cyber power	The extent to which the cyber action of an individual or an organization or a nation state is likely to facilitate its achieving its objectives. A high level of cyber power implies access to state of the art technology and a high level of competence in this field. However due to the asymmetric nature of cyber power the biggest entities may not necessarily be the most powerful.

Term	Definition
Cyber power index	A measure of an organization's or a national state's capability within cyberspace. It includes hardware, software and expertise.
Cyber propaganda	The use of computers and networks to disseminate a biased message. Cyber propaganda can be conducted using publicly available social software products such as Facebook and Twitter. It may be targeted at groups or at individuals.
Cyber raid	A quick short lived cyber attack. It may be conducted as a proof of concept to establish the vulnerability of a set of cyber assets.
Cyber reconnaissance	The process of learning about the vulnerability of one's opponent's computers and networks in order to establish a strategy for attack or for defense.
Cyber Red Teaming (CRT)	A group of individuals whose purpose is to attack a computer or network as part of a testing or training exercise. The color red is used to indicate an adversary.
Cyber resilience	The ability of a computer system or network to recover from a cyber attack that it has experienced. It is sometimes argued that, as cyber attacks are now inevitable, cyber resilience has become the key issue in ensuring business continuity for any organization civil or military. Cyber resilience policies need to be carefully planned well before there is any question of an attack.
Cyber resilient architecture	In cyberspace the term architecture normally refers to the configuration of the cyber assets that are in place in order to achieve the organization's objectives. Resilience refers to how

Term	Definition
	well and how quickly a computer or network's functionality can be recovered after a cyber attack. A cyber resilient architecture is one which has been created with the view to being able to prevent any damage occurring from a cyber attack and in the event of an attacker breaking through the cyber defenses being able to continue functioning, despite the cyber attack. A key element in this architecture is the assets required for a rapid recovery to a full state of functionality after an attack has occurred.
Cyber risk assessment	An evaluation of the probability of the actual occurrence of the risks to which a computer system or a network is prone. A risk assessment should list all feasible risks as well as a statement of the potential damage which would accrue to the organization, if the risk was realized. Risk assessments often also deals with actions which would be required in order to mitigate the damage which would occur in event of the risk materializing.
Cyber sabotage	Sabotage is an act of deliberate damage or obstruction to a system. It is often the objective of an act of sabotage to prevent an occurrence from taking place or to ensure that an individual does not achieve his or her objectives. This is regarded as a disruptive cyber attack as opposed to a destructive attack.
Cyber security	Cyber security begins with the awareness that computers and networks are vulnerable. Its central theme is a concern about ensuring that no harm comes to any of an organizations cyber assets. Cyber security involves being aware of the ways in which a computer or network can be

Term	Definition
	damaged by both a deliberate attack and also by accidental events. An important part of cyber security is to inform all those who work with the system as to what the potential threats are and how they should behave in order to minimize these threats. Cyber security also addresses the issue of resilience so that if a cyber attack occurs and the systems are damaged the organization can quickly recover. Cyber security requires the organization to have a clearly articulated policy which is carefully implemented and regularly policed.
Cyber security appliances	Cyber security appliances are both hardware and software devices whose purpose is to enhance the probability that no harm comes to the organization's cyber assets. The range of devices is substantial and includes antivirus software, closed-circuit television, biometric scanning as well as appropriate cabinets and safes into which backup copies of software and data are lodged.
Cyber security leadership	Leadership is a complex issue which involves having a clear view and being prepared to state forcibly. It also involves being fully aware of all the relevant circumstances and being able to propose appropriate solutions to problems. Cyber security leadership has been described as the quality of being able to influence others and to engage them in constructive thinking with regards to the range of issues encompassed by cyber security. Cyber security is not always perceived as being a critical issue for individuals or organizations or nation states. However, in the past few years there has been an increasing number of cyber crimes and violations across

Term	Definition
	cyberspace so that the issue is now recognized as being of significant importance and it is most likely that will become more important in the near future.
Cyber stalking	The ability to use cyber products to continually monitor the location and the activities of individuals. Stalking implies more than simple observing as it is unwanted monitoring, which includes some degree of annoyance to the individual being stalked.
Cyber stress test	A cyber stress test determines the key aspects of a system which are the most vulnerable in terms of physical devices (hardware and software), people and locations.
Cyber surveillance	The use of a variety of tools to monitor traffic on the Internet. This includes reading and listening to messages and conversations without the knowledge let alone the authorization of the individuals involved.
Cyber target	The person or organization to be harmed by a cyber attack. Sometimes a cyber attack can be aimed at an individual as with an attempted fraud or it can be aimed at an organization when a Denial of Service attack is being perpetrated. The target can also be a group of organizations such as occurred with the ransom attack on NHS hospitals in the UK in 2017.
Cyber terrorism	Whether something is an act of terrorism is largely a matter of perspective. Traditionally terrorism is an act of violence conducted outside the formal state of war. This act of violence frequently involves considerable indiscriminate collateral damage. The essence of terrorism is

Term	Definition
	that it delivers a high degree of fear (terror) to a wide range of people who include noncombatants. It is also typically aimed at non-military targets such as cinemas and restaurants or in recent times people walking in the streets.
	It is the fact that terrorist activities have become so indiscriminate with regards to whom they injure that has made them so repugnant, as well as the fact that terrorist attacks are an affront to the authority of the nation state.
	In cyberspace the attack on a nuclear power station or an air traffic control system would be seen as cyber terrorism, as it would engender a high degree of fear or terror in the population, and could result in a large amount of indiscriminate collateral damage.
Cyber theft	The unlawful appropriation of cyber assets. This could include hardware and software as well as data. Cyber theft can be committed locally such as the copying of a data file onto a memory stick and the removal of that memory stick from the premises of the data's owner, or it could involve theft over the Internet whereby the data is stolen by a remote agent at a different location and perhaps in a different country or continent. Much of what is described as software piracy can also be called cyber theft.
Cyber threat	Any hostile or potentially hostile activity which may do harm to any aspect of cyberspace or any of the individuals, organizations or nation states who are participating in the use thereof.
	Threats are as much a matter of perception as anything else. In order to be able to create and

Term	Definition
	actualize a cyber risk reduction policy it is necessary to be able to envisage all possible cyber threats and their possible implications.
Cyber threat intelligence framework	Cyber threat intelligence is the output of the collection of relevant data an organization has available for analysis and interpretation. To make this possible it is necessary to have a framework within which all the activities associated with threat analysis are understood and thereby given meaning. Cyber threat intelligence is also sometimes described as a way of understanding information received about the threats which your cyber assets are facing.
Cyber traffic analysis	In cyberspace traffic analysis examines communication patterns between different entities on the web or using Internet communications. It involves the intercepting and examining of messages from which it deduces patterns or relationships.
Cyber treaties	Attempts to find agreement between nation states with regards to the avoidance of conflict in cyberspace and the establishment of a common approach to cyber crime.
Cyber trespass	The act of obtaining access to a computer system or network for which one is not properly authorized. This may be done physically by the intruder sitting behind a terminal at a desk where he or she is not permitted, or it can be done remotely through a communications network such as the Internet. Attacks on websites which change the original content can be seen as acts of cyber trespass as well as cyber vandalism.

Term	Definition
Cyber utopianism	The view that cyber activities are essentially beneficial to humanity and that their use will lead to a better society for all. A cyber utopian would not acknowledge that there is a downside to cyberspace but would only emphasize the positive side of the technology and its application. With the increase in cyber crime and the use of the technology in nefarious ways, it has become increasingly difficult to defend this cyber utopian point of view as it is now recognized that there needs to be some control over how both cyber activities and the data on which these are based, should be controlled.
Cyber vandalism	Vandalism is a wide-ranging word which describes deliberate damage to public or private property. One of the characteristics of vandalism is that there is often no apparent gain to be had by the perpetrator. The harm done to the victim is the only motive for this course of action. In certain circumstances vandalism is considered as a lesser form of crime, than an outright attack. In the cyberspace the defacing of websites would generally be considered an act of cyber vandalism. It has been argued that teenage hackers who have broken into established websites such as government departments or banks or credit card companies should be regarded as vandals. Not surprisingly the owners of these websites have not always agreed with this view and cyber vandals have been prosecuted in courts of law.

Term	Definition
Cyber vetting	The idea of cyber vetting is primarily that a potential employer can consult the digital footprint of a prospective employee in order to obtain further information about an individual's behavior or personality.
Cyber war combatants	Any individual, organization, or nation state which engages in acts of cyber warfare. Cyber war combatants are mostly covert and difficult to identify.
Cyber warfare	The notion of cyber warfare is contested in the sense that it has been argued that it can only occur after a cyber war has been declared or when cyber warfare antagonist's actions have been clearly identified and owned. Furthermore, the term warfare implies that the nation states or their direct agents are involved with the attack. However, what is more generally considered to be cyber warfare occurs without any declaration of war and it is often not completely clear who the perpetrators are. No nation state at the time of writing has overtly declared a cyber war on another nation state, so thus far no overt or openly declared cyber war has actually occurred. It is sometimes extraordinary difficult to prove who was, in fact, the originator of a cyber attack. Included in this difficulty is the question of what evidence is necessary and sufficient to constitute proof of the source of an attack and under whose jurisdiction action should be taken.
Cyber warfare dimensions	There are said to be four dimensions to cyber warfare which are Active, Passive, Physical and Cognitive. An active attack results in data or software having been changed or harmed. A passive attack involves something like eaves-

Term	Definition
	dropping or event data being stolen. A physical attack involves physical harm of some sort such as damage to assets. A cognitive attack causes the perception of people to be changed. The Russian intervention in the USA Presidential election in 2016 has been referred to as a cognitive attack.
Cyber weapons	The range of weaponized malware which can be used across the Internet to harm opponent's computer and network systems. The term is not usually used in connection with cyber criminal activity such as phishing, nor with general cyber abuse such as cyber bullying.
Cyberchondria	The tendency for individuals who have health concerns to research their symptoms on the Internet and to attempt to make sense of technical health material without the assistance of health professionals. The result of this is said to have led to a higher number of visits to medical practitioners and for the patients to demand specialized health treatments, which have at least in some cases been regarded as unnecessary and perhaps even harmful.
Cybermetrics	Measures which indicate how well cyber devices and cyber systems and those who use them are performing in the achievement of their objectives. *See Webometrics.*
Cyberpunk	A genre of science fiction, the origins of which are rooted back in the 1960s and 1970s.
Cyberspace	In its broadest sense cyberspace is the domain in which all data is captured, stored, transferred, manipulated and distributed in such a way as to

Term	Definition
	optimize its usefulness to individuals, organizational and nation states.
	Cyberspace not only includes the Internet and world wide web but also the storing of data on large optical devices and even on memory sticks. It includes physical and intellectual dimensions incorporating the law as it pertains to cyber assets and their use as well as the human resources which employ them.
Cyberspace Operations (CO)	A military term related to a specific sector of the wider information domain in which the military takes an active interest and also performs its tasks. Cyberspace operations is perceived as one of the capabilities under the more general heading of information operations and concerns all activities in which there is an active role for cyber assets. *See Information operations.*
Cyberspace superiority	Either the real or perceived advantage one entity has over another with regards to the quality or extent of their ICT or cyber ability. It is sometimes argued that any notion of cyberspace superiority is illusionary because even in a non-technologically developed country, it is possible for an individual to create malware and launch a cyber attack with minimal cyber infrastructure. This has been referred to as a leveling of the cyber warfare field.

D

Dark web to Dummy system

Term	Definition
Dark web	A part of the World Wide Web which is not normally accessible through commonly used search engines. Dark Websites are not indexed by search engines. It is estimated that the dark Web may contain as much as five times more material as a surface web which is a term now used to describe all other web activities other than the dark Web itself. The Dark Web is said to be the domain of nefarious organizations and activities where drugs weapons and other illegal entities are allegedly traded. However, there are apologists for the Dark Web, who believe that its use should not be discouraged, as it provides means by which individuals can anonymously exchange information and ideas without any third party surveillance.
Data breach	When data security systems and procedures have been circumvented by any unauthorized entity, the data is said to have been breached. Breaching a computer system can be an intensively technological exercise, although this is not always the case, as people can leave systems vulnerable through ignorance or neglect. A data breach can also occur due to non-technological blunders such as the case of a government employee leaving a CD on a seat on a train which happened a few years ago in the UK.

Term	Definition
Data diddling	(Also known as false data entry) is a form of deception/ falsification used by person trying to forge/counterfeit documents by changing data before or during entry into a computer system and then changing it back after the processing is completed.
Data exfiltration	This term may be used in a couple of different ways. Data exfiltration can describe the ability of malware to extricate itself from data files, normally after it has initiated harm or damage to the data, and in so doing cover up its exit trail. The term can also be used to describe the unauthorized transfer or duplication of data from one system to another. It can be conducted "manually" by an individual present at a computer (for example using a data stick) or it can be accomplished over a computer network.
Data fidelity	Data Fidelity refers to the authenticity of the data, which in turn deals with how well the data delivers a proper reflection of what it purports to. This requires the data to be error free, accurate, complete and relatively free from bias.
Data leakage	An unauthorized release of data from a computer or network. It may be as simple as facts and figures being release verbally by an employee without permission or it could be the theft of data storage devices or the illegal hacking into a computer network.
Data mining	The practice of extracting previously unseen insights including patterns, connections, correlations etc. from large pre-existing databases, in order to generate new information.

Term	Definition
Data preparation	The work necessary before a set of data can be accepted for processing in a computer. It may be simply the requirement to check the data to ensure that it is valid, or it may involve converting data from one format to another. Data preparation can involve data cleaning which requires errors to be extracted or amended in the data. This constitutes a significant amount of work requiring significant human resources.
Data protection act	Many countries have specific legislation with regards to how individuals' personal data are acquired, stored, and used. Legislation pertaining to these issues in the UK is referred to as the Data Protection Act. Different names are used for this type of legislation in other countries.
Data validation	Procedures which are put in place in order to ensure that data is checked for its authenticity, relevance or accuracy before it is accepted or even entered into a computer system. There is a range of techniques available to ensure that the number of mistakes made at the point of data entry is minimized. *See Data preparation.*
Deep learning	In the pedagogical sense deep learning refers to the application of knowledge acquired over time about which there has been material reflection. In cyberspace however, deep learning, which is sometimes called deep structured learning and machine learning, has been produced by complex technology often involving neural networks. In this case there is supervised and unsupervised learning. The learning models are based on an artificial neural network.

Term	Definition
Deep web	The portion of the web which is not indexed by search engines. The deep web consists of all the proprietary databases which use Internet and web technology and which are not open to the general public. The deep web has nothing to do with the dark web.
Defense cyber operation	Activities undertaken by individuals, organizations, and nation states to defend their cyber assets from attack by anyone. Activities which have the aim of preventing any cyber attack and of limiting the adverse effects if any such cyber attack should occur.
Deniability	Arrangements made by fraudsters or those initiating a cyber attack so that their actions will either be untraceable or if they are discovered they will be in a position to deny responsibility.
Denial of Service (DoS)	A cyber attack which overloads a computer or a computer network to such an extent that it is unable to cope with the volume of activity that has been presented and therefore the computer or computer network fails to function. Effectively the capacity of the system is overwhelmed with a flood of Internet traffic which causes a "traffic jam". The service which the system was intended to offer legitimate users is no longer available which the attack persists. *See Distributed denial of service*
Detection capability	The ability of a computer or network system to sense that an attack is underway.
Deterrence	Deterrence refers to the ability of a target to discourage an attack, normally because of the consequences of retaliation.

Term	Definition
Didactic training	Training offered in the form of traditional courses and learning sessions. This is sometimes referred to as "teacher centered training." It is contrasted with experiential or activity learning.
Digital	Originating from the word "digit" which besides meaning a number from 0 to 9 also has the meaning of a finger or a toe, digital refers to the characteristics of a device which are based on modern computer technology. This technology is based on electronic components which use logic underpinned by binary expressions. A digital device will normally have a display or readout rather than a dial with a pointer or hand as in the case of a watch. The mechanism for controlling a digital device will be based on computer technology which today will be increasingly connected to the Internet and will use data and logic as primary instruments for its control. As a result of the connection to data and the Internet the expressions digital strategy, digital activism, and digital excellence have become part of modern vocabulary.
Digital footprint	As each individual's Internet enabled devices and services are used, so he or she leaves an electronic trace behind with regards to what they have been doing. Thus the use of the search engine Google leaves a record of the items which were searched. The use of a smart phone leaves a trail of the people and institutions that were phoned. Furthermore, Internet services such as Facebook and YouTube invite users to express their opinions by clicking on the like or dislike icons. Such expressions of opinion are

Term	Definition
	registered in the record of the activity of the user, and may be understood as representing the "personality" of the individual involved.
Digital forensics	The word forensic is derived from the Latin word for Forum where the Roman Court of Law was held. The term forensic refers to an investigation of a crime or something which is suspected of being a crime. This is done in such a way that the evidence can be presented to a Court of Law. Digital forensics is such an investigation using digital evidence or it could be the investigation of a crime which has been committed using digital technology.
Digital life	At one level, digital life is another way of talking about digital footprint. Also the term Digital life refers to work being carried out on the interface between computers and people which is commonly referred to as Human – Computer Interaction or HCI. The goal of research in this area is to improve the effectiveness by which computers may be used in a number of different professional and private capacities.
Digital manipulation	The alteration of any cyber record in order to mislead. A popular way of digital manipulation is through the use of products such as Photoshop.
Digital native	A digital native is an individual who has grown up in the so-called digital age. This suggests that the person concerned will have learnt about how to use cyber devices from an early age. This is to be contrasted with others who have learnt about computers, the Internet and other cyber devices as adults. It is suggested that digital natives have a much more profound and intuitive

Term	Definition
	understanding of all aspects of cyberspace. This term digital native has been in use since the late 1990s.
Digital shadow	A synonym for digital footprint. *See Digital footprint.*
Digital sovereignty	The term has a number of possible different meanings, but all of them refer to the rights of some entity over their behavior in cyberspace or their web presence. Digital Sovereignty normally refers to the right to capture, store, forward and use data. In former times the issue of storage was less complicated as data was normally stored on a local device attached to a computer. With the arrival of cloud computing this is no longer the case and the location of data storage is not easy to identify. It is not always clear where data is now actually stored. It has been suggested that this is contrary to one of the principles of data sovereignty which suggests that data should be stored within the country of the owner of the data. Digital Sovereignty may also refer to an individual's right over their digital representation in society.
Digital strategy	The way in which an entity uses cyber assets to achieve its objectives. Individuals, organizations and nation states can have a digital strategy.
Dirty tricks	In most situations there are what are commonly regarded as accepted behavior parameters within which all actors even opponents should operate. Actions which are not regarded as being entirely

Term	Definition
	moral or ethical and normally undertaken in a surreptitious manner in order to put a competitor or an adversary at a disadvantage are referred to as dirty tricks.
Disinformation	Similar to fake news and fake information this term is also used to indicate a disbelief or out-right denial of whatever legitimate information is being offered.
Dissidents and the dark web	Activities in the dark web are regarded as being anonymous and therefore it is suggested that it is a safe place for dissidents to express their opinions which might otherwise lead to their prosecution.
Distributed Denial of Service (DDoS)	This is a cyber attack which overloads a computer network resulting in legitimate users of the network being unable to access the service which the network normally provides them. A DDoS is based on the dispatching of a large number, perhaps thousands or tens of thousands, of phony or fictitious requests for access to a website. The computer becomes so engaged in handling these fictitious requests, that it is unable to cope with the normal legitimate traffic for which the system was intended.
Downside	The possible outcome of the situation, often negative, when and where circumstances intervene and the stated objectives are not all achieved. The downside is when things go wrong. The opposite of the downside is sometimes said to be the upside potential. The downside of the use of cyber assets is not often addressed.

Term	Definition
Dropping USB drives attack	Inappropriately accessing a computer network by setting a trap for an unsuspecting employee. This is a form of social engineering cyber attack whereby a memory stick is dropped in a public place with the intention that a passer-by will pick it up and attempt to use it. In doing so a cyber attack is launched. *See Social engineering cyber attack.*
Dual purpose	The facility by which a product or a system or some other entity can have two uses. Often used to refer to a product that has both civilian and military purposes.
Dummy system	An apparent system which attracts a cyber attack thereby distracting the attacker from the intended target. Dummy systems are used as a decoy in order to avert an attack on the real system.

e-Activism to Exploitation route

Term	Definition
e-Activism	There are a number of different ways this term can be used. It can be a reference to the use of cyberspace by traditional activists who are interested in promoting their cause using this technology. They may be promoting better road safety, diet, or hygiene in schools for example. The term can also be used to describe how individuals and/or organizations have taken it upon themselves to try to influence cyber policy at the local, regional national or international level.
e-Commerce	The use of Internet technology to facilitate business transactions. E-Commerce has changed the face of retailing and has been responsible for the reduction in the number of High Street retail outlets. E-Commerce is now widespread in Business to Consumer (B2C) relationships, as well as Business to Business (B2B) and Business to Government (B2G). It has also changed the way in which travel arrangements are conducted with online airline reservations and hotel bookings to mention only two aspects. e-Commerce has been responsible for the creation and success of many business organizations such as Amazon, e-Bay and UBER.

Term	Definition
Economic cost of cyber security	The creating of cyber security policies and the implementation thereof takes time and money and therefore has an economic cost. This cost can be substantial. However, if a cyber attack is successful, considerable damage can be done to not only the cyber assets but to the organization itself. It is important to ensure that cyber security policies do not incur greater cost than would be experienced if the cyber threat were to materialize. Although this principle is clear it can be difficult to estimate the economic cost of a successful cyber attack.
Economic ecosystem	This term could be a euphemism for what economists would refer to as the marketplace. However, this would suggest that there are many more variables involved than simply the price mechanism which is normally the sole or at least the dominant focus of free-market economists.
Economic information warfare	The struggle to obtain superior information among competitors in the economic marketplace. This may include individuals, business and corporations or nation states.
Economic warfare	A range of activities related to competitive struggles in the market place. This can be related to price cutting or racing for new product development or offering potential customers new and better terms of trade. The term warfare is used here in an allegoric sense. It could also refer to sanctions or blockades during kinetic warfare. Another element in economic warfare could be what is referred to as dumping, which involves the offering of subsidies or bounties to industries in order to make

Term	Definition
	their products or services more competitive on the international markets.
e-Democracy	The application of Internet technology to try to make democractic processes more efficient and more accessible to a greater part of the society. There are many possible applications which come under the heading of e-Democracy including e-Voting, e-Canvassing, e-Participation, e-Consultation etc. One of the major criticisms of e-Democracy is that only individuals with access to the Internet will have the opportunity of using the facilities offered by the technology.
Effect assessment	Effect assessment tries to answer the question, "how satisfactory has the outcome been?" It is an attempt to attribute value to the result of creating, acquiring operating or abandoning a system or a policy. It is often a judgment call on the performance of an investment or on the operation of those who have initiated the systems or policies being assessed. It is a central part of any system operation.
e-Government	The application of Internet based technology to improve government services. It involves many possible systems including government to citizen (G2C) as well as government to business (G2B) and government to government (G2G) applications. In some cases, e-Government has reduced the cost of public services and has also reduced waiting lists. Sometimes the term e-Governance is also used as a synonym for the e-Government.
Electronic warfare	Using focused energy, which includes radio waves or laser light, electronic warfare is concerned with confusing and disabling an enemy's

Term	Definition
	electronics. Electronic warfare can also be employed for listening. This may involve collecting radio signals from the enemy or sensing the radar of an incoming missile. In the context of cyberspace electronic warfare is largely synonymous with cyber warfare or digital warfare.
Embedded training	Training which is integrated into the way an organization functions. It has also been referred to as active learning. This type of training happens routinely during the working experience without the necessity of having to attend formal classroom sessions.
Emotional damage	Emotional damage is harm done to individuals which is not always immediately visible or obvious. Individuals who have been scammed often assert that not only have they been cheated out of financial resources, but that they have also experienced emotional damage caused by the unpleasant experience. In some cases their self esteem is reduced while in other cases they become more fearful of anything unfamiliar in their environment. This is especially the case when a substantial amount of money has been stolen from elderly individuals who are often the target of scams.
Encrypted app	This is a cyber application which has been protected by the use of some form of encryption technology in order to prevent it from being accessed or used by unauthorized individuals.
Encrypted connection	An approach to ensure security when transferring data. When two or more cyber devices are used to exchange information that has been encrypted, it is an encrypted connection.

Term	Definition
Encryption	The process of coding a communication in such a way that it can only be understood by authorized parties who have been given access to the necessary instructions to decode the communication. It can protect messages if unauthorized individuals attempt to intercept them. Encryption underpins most financial transactions across the Internet.
End-to-end Encryption	An approach to coding and decoding electronic messages which is intended to ensure that no third party can intercept a message and understand it. It is designed to prevent surveillance or tampering with data transmission.
Enemy	An entity, a person, an organization or a nation state whose intention is to do harm to the interests of another party. Relationships with enemies, like friendships, can be temporary, as individuals and organizations can change sides.
Ethical hackers	Ethical or white hat hackers are "good guys". In order to make sure that cyber systems are as secure as possible, some organizations have employed highly skilled individuals to attempt to hack into their systems. The objective of ethical or white hat hacking is to strengthen cyber security defenses.
EU 1 hour rule	There are proposals made by the European Commission that social media platforms like Facebook and Twitter should be obliged to remove offensive material within one hour of it being reported.
Europay, Mastercard, Visa (EMV)	The technology employed in chip and PIN credit/debit card validation.

Term	Definition
Evil twin attacks	An evil twin attack occurs in a public WiFi space where fraudsters set up a phony or fake WiFi Hot Spot connection, which is almost a perfect copy of an already established legal WiFi supplier. The system is arranged in such a way that the target thinks that he or she is connecting to a legitimate public WiFi service, when in fact, they are being asked to supply their details to fraudsters. This type of scam is usually perpetrated in restaurants or hotels or other public places.
Exfiltration	*See Data exfiltration.*
Exploitation	In the cyberspace context, exploitation refers to the taking advantage of security vulnerabilities, in order to attack a system. It could also refer to videos taken of children without their consent as well as individuals being blackmailed because of explicit videos having been taken of them.
Exploitation risk	The possibility of a system being subjected to a cyber attack may be described as its exploitation risk. No matter how good the defense systems are an exploitation risk is never zero.
Exploitation route/ attack path/ infiltration point	The series of actions which an attacker needs to perform in order to be able to get access to the system under attack. This consists of selecting a particular event on the attack surface and following the necessary steps to penetrate the system in order to arrive at the desired target. There can be many steps in the exploitation route and it can take considerable time (weeks, months or even years) and much effort to achieve the objectives of the proposed attack.

Face profile scams to Freenet

Term	Definition
Face profile scams	The use of pictures of individuals by scammers to hide their identity. The photographs can be of professional models which are then used in romance scams to endear the scammer to his or her target. The individual whose face is used generally does not have any knowledge of the scam.
Facebook	Launched in 2004 Facebook is the leading social software product which now claims to have about 2 billion users. Because of its size and its long standing in the marketplace it has much of the characteristics of a monopoly. Facebook has recently come under severe criticism for allowing personal data of some of its members to be used for the purposes of political canvassing.
Facebook profiling	The use of data acquired from Facebook members in order to categorize them in terms of their potential to hold certain opinions and to be susceptible to different types of advertising messages. The initial purpose of Facebook profiling was to market goods and services. Using profile data advertisers selling specific types of goods and services would focus on particular individuals. However, recently this type of profiling has also been used by political parties in order to maximize the impact of their political messages in an attempt to increase their share of the vote.

Term	Definition
Facebook removals	Facebook will remove postings for a number of reasons including copyright infringements, the posting of violent, and other illegal material. It has been argued that Facebook has been slow in removing offensive material and that it should not allow such material to be posted in the first place. Facebook has resounded that it is not in the business of censorship. This argument is ongoing.
Fake blocking notices	A mocked up document which will inform a user that unless an amount of money is paid, or unless an account number or password is entered into a computer some service will be terminated.

A faked blocking notice is a means of initiating the extortion of money or the unlawful acquisition of identity details. |
| **Fake data** | Data which purports to be genuine but which is in fact fictitious. Fake data is usually a euphemism for misrepresentations or simply lies.

Anyone who accepts fake data as being correct is being misled. |
| **Fake news** | In the simplest terms fake news is a euphemism for a lie. It may be described as any communication undertaken by any form of the media which purports to report on factual events or accurately repeat opinions but which does not represent what actually happened or what was said.

Fake news may take various forms including outright deceptions to news presented with a particular bias. The omission of important facts may be regarded as creating fake news. Fake |

Term	Definition
	news is not a new phenomenon but has come to prominence recently in the political area especially in the USA. In the UK what was first described during Prime Minister Blair's premiership as political spin could be today regarded as fake news. However, the term fake news used in the political community can often simply be a slur to discredit what is actually genuine news.
Fake WiFi hot Spots	These are traps which have been created by fraudsters in order to lull unexpected users into providing them with user IDs and passwords. They appear on the computers users screen as though they are the typical WiFi hotspots encountered in cafes, restaurants and hotels while in fact they are actually instruments to defraud the public. *See Evil twin attack.*
Fanboys	Someone who is excessively enthusiastic and of the male gender.
Fancy bear	Identified as a cyber espionage group associated with the Russian GRU (this is the English version of a Russian acronym meaning the Main Intelligence Directorate) group. *See Cozy Bear.*
Field bus network/protocol	A family of communication protocols used for the automation of processes related to various types of industrial processes.
Firewall	In cyberspace a firewall is a network security system which protects a computer or a network of computers from cyber attacks.

Term	Definition
Flickr	An online photo and video sharing social media platform.
Freedom of the Press Foundation	A USA 501(c)3 non-profit organization dedicated to helping support and defend public interest journalism focused on exposing mismanagement, corruption, and law breaking in government. The Foundation works to preserve and strengthen the rights guaranteed to the press under the First Amendment through crowdfunding, digital security and internet advocacy.
Freenet	Established in 2000, Freenet is a peer-to-peer platform with strong privacy connectivity.

G

GCHQ to Guerrilla open access manifesto

Term	Definition
GCHQ	GCHQ stands for the Government Communications Headquarters and is a facility in the UK that protects the country from cyber attacks. It is regarded as the UK's most secret agency.
General Data Protection Regulation (GDPR)	The General Data Protection Regulation is part of EU law on data protection and privacy for all individuals within the EU and the EEA. The GDPR aims primarily to give control to citizens and residents over their personal data. A major update of GDPR took place in May 2018.
General Morphological Analysis (GMA)	GMA is a method for exploring all the possible solutions to a multi-dimensional, non-quantified complex problem.
Geneva protocol	A protocol for the prohibition of the use in war of asphyxiating, poisonous or other gases, as well as bacteriological methods of warfare. The protocol prohibits the use of chemical and biological weapons in war under the auspices of the League of Nations.
Global Commission on the Stability of Cyberspace (GCSC)	Based in The Hague, the GCSC was initiated by two independent think tanks, The Hague Centre for Strategic Studies (HCSS) and the EastWest Institute (EWI). It helps promote mutual awareness and understanding across international cyberspace communities.

Term	Definition
Global pandemic	An outbreak of infectious disease that has spread across a large region, possibly the whole world. The word pandemic should be contrasted with epidemic which refers to an outbreak of a disease which attacks many people at about the same time, but which is relatively geographically contained within one or a few communities. Some cyber attacks may be considered as a global pandemic phenomenon.
Go viral	Becoming very popular by circulating quickly from person to person through the Internet.
Google report card	A report of the products and services offered by Google.
Government surveillance programs	For security purposes governments have a variety of surveillance projects which range from listening into telephone calls to reading emails to observing patterns of behavior of individuals. These are generally under the direct control of the national security services.
Graphical spam	Spam filters are efficient at blocking text spams by identifying words which are regularly used by spammers. However, this technique does not work with images and thus there has been a shift to spam containing graphical images.
Grey hat	A hacker who is not necessarily out to harm a computer system but who has not been specifically employed by an interested party to help identify and eliminate computer of network vulnerability. Grey hats are independent and cannot be relied upon in the struggle against cybercrime.

Term	Definition
Guerilla open access manifesto	This manifesto was written in the USA at the time of the struggle to obtain free access to academic journals. Written by free information activist Aaron Schwartz the manifesto opposed the high cost of obtaining the knowledge which is published in expensive academic journals. It has been argued that the Guerilla Open Access Manifesto prompted the prosecution services in Boston to request a tough punishment for Aaron Schwartz when he was prosecuted for downloading academic journal articles.

H

Hacked mail server to Hybrid warfare

Term	Definition
Hacked mail server	A mail server which has been compromised by a cyber attack and which will function or appear to function in order to further the ends of the attacker. Very often this involves sending out large amounts of spam to individuals. This spam may or may not contain viruses or other malware.
Hacker	The term hack proceeds the computer age and was used to describe someone who did repetitive and sometimes rough and unskilled work. It was often used in the sense of writing not particularly interesting material.
	In the context of cyberspace, a hacker, is an individual who obtains access to a computer or a network without proper authority. Hackers range from schoolchildren to gangsters to agents of hostile governments. Hacking is in many countries a criminal offence.
	However, there is a class of hackers who are acceptable and these are individuals employed by organizations to test the robustness of their security systems. These individuals are referred to as ethical or white hat hackers. Some sources say that all other hackers should be referred to as black hat hackers. Occasionally reference is made to grey hat hackers who are individuals whose intentions are not entirely clear. They

Term	Definition
	may simply be pitting their wits against the system for the sake of the intellectual challenge of overcoming the obstacles created by the systems defenders.
Hacker warfare	The struggle between white hat and black hat hackers. This has also been referred to as an intellectual arms race whereby those who wish to cause damage to computers and networks match their skills against those who are defending the systems.
Hackers congress	A meeting of Hackers convened by the Institute of Cyberanarchy.
Hacking	A term used to describe the activities the person (i.e. the Hacker) uses to gain access to a computer or network. *See Hacker.*
Hacktivism	Hacking is sometimes seen as a digital equivalent of trespassing or even burglary. However, the phenomenon of hacking can also have a more sinister connotation. Hacktivism suggests the use of cyber devices in a subversive way to promote a political agenda. Although in many cases hacktivism has been associated with groups advocating free speech, human rights and freedom of information, there are also those who regard it as being more closely associated with forms of cyber terrorism.
Hacktivist	At one level this term is used to describe an individual involved in the processes of hacking. However, it is also used as a label in the context of more sinister Internet activities to describe someone who is involved in hacktivism.

Term	Definition
Hashtag	Used on social networks it is a method of creating a user-generated flag which makes it possible for others to easily find messages with a specific theme or content.
Hate mail	Messages transmitted and received over the Internet intended to belittle, threaten or abuse an individual. It is often unclear as to what extent hate mail is illegal rather than unacceptable. Hate mail is a significant aspect of cyber bullying. Despite much debate as to how hate mail can be eliminated or at least minimized, there is currently no clear solution to this problem.
Hidden wikis	Websites which employ wiki type technology but are not available on the surface Internet. To access these websites it is necessary to use the deep web or the dark web.
Honey tokens	Fictitious data which are added to a database to distract cyber intruders. They are effectively decoys off which a cyber attack will be deflected. They are especially useful as part of a cyber defense strategy.
Honeypot	A computer security mechanism designed to detect and deflect cyber attacks on a computer system or network. A honeypot usually consists of data which appears to be genuine and of value to an attacker, but which has actually been isolated from the real system and is of little value. Thus any cyber attack is isolated and contained.
Https	Hypertext Transfer Protocol Secure. It is the secure transit of data through a secure socket layer (SSL) or transport layer security (TLS) protocol connection.

Term	Definition
Hybrid threats	A hybrid threat arises from the potential of harm coming from different sources or different techniques. In cyberspace this could refer to both threats which arise from across the Internet, and threats which originate from individuals working within the organization. The actualization of this type of threat involving insiders and outsiders is now being referred to as a blended cyber attack.
Hybrid warfare	It is now generally accepted that warfare may be conducted in 5 theatres i.e. land, sea, air, space and cyberspace. Hybrid warfare can combine operations in any or all of these of these arenas and thus it may use multiple weapons, resources and tactics to attack the enemy.

I

IBM Watson to IP address

Term	Definition
IBM Watson	A state of the art AI application developed by International Business Machine Inc (IBM).
	It involves various aspects of machine learning, neural networks, and voice recognition and performs at speeds which are normally not associated with these types of applications.
	IBM Watson is famous for having beaten expert human contestants on the TV show Jeopardy.
Identity	The identity of an individual is how he or she is differentiated from anyone else. It is a statement of who that person is. An individual's identity is established by confirming a number of facts describing that person. The primary source is a name. In countries where all citizens are registered with the state there is often a Social Security or National Health Number which is also a primary dimension of identity. Other important aspects of identity are date of birth, gender, physical characteristics, languages spoken, residential address, and profession.
Identity theft	The illegal appropriation of personal information with the intention of using it to fraudulently misrepresent the victim, whose identity has been stolen and by so doing acquire goods and/or services at the expense of the victim.

Term	Definition
If you are not paying	A principle which is being continually articulated since the Cambridge Analytica revelations that by using a useful application that is free, then the collection of user data is a primary objective of the application and it will be monetized. In this context user data not only refers to details which the user has supplied to the system such as those elicited by Facebook, but also information with regards to the preferences of the user which may be indicated through the *like* or *dislike* buttons. This type of information can be used to create psychological profiles of the user group.
Illegal downloads	The extraction of data from any source without the necessary permissions, is regarded as theft, and is in many countries a violation of the law of the land. However, one of the problems faced by the cyber community is that it is not always clear where the jurisdiction lies from the point of view of taking action against the illegal download. An illegal download can be initiated from almost anywhere and the data or software stolen can likewise be sent to virtually any destination.
Incident response	The reaction to an incident which in cyberspace is normally a cyber attack.
Incident response team	The group of people whose responsibility it is to react to a cyber attack or incident. An incident response team is regarded as a central part of any cyber security program.
Industrial Control Systems (ICS)	The different kinds of control systems used to operate an industrial and manufacturing process. ICS function in many industries ranging from chemicals, energy, transport, mining to mention

Term	Definition
	only a few. They always entail both digital devices and physical machinery of some sort. ICS have increased the efficiency of production and have also been in a number of cases responsible for a reduction in hazards to workmen.
Infographics	Visual aids that present information to the reader or viewer clearly and quickly to enhance the topic. If a picture is worth 1000 words then infographics is at the heart of any efficient and effective program of communications.
Information	Traditionally information was said to have been the product of processing data. Russell Ackoff postulated a *data, information, knowledge, wisdom* hierarchy as a representation of how we came to understand the world about us. In this model information was processed or organized data. However, the model has been the subject of considerable debate for a number of reasons. Firstly, there are many overlaps concerning what is thought of as being data and information and these two concepts are now seen as being virtually interchangeable. To add to this there is difficulty with the definition of knowledge as once again it can be hard to see the boundaries between information and knowledge, and the concept of wisdom is also highly problematical.
Information assurance	Information presented to an individual or organization should never be automatically assumed to be correct. All organizations have to face the question of how accurate, reliable and valid the information is that they have at their disposal. Therefore procedures are put in place to ensure the integrity of information, described under the heading of information assurance.

Term	Definition
Information confrontation	When different accounts are presented about a situation this can be described as information confrontation. It is always important to understand how information confrontation takes place and to resolve any ambiguities which may arise there from. Information Confrontation can be seen as a tool of cyber warfare, but it can also occur in non-conflict situations.
Information deterrence	How information can be employed in a program to deter acts of cyber warfare or cyber criminality. One of the central issues of information deterrence is to inform potential offenders that if they commit an unacceptable act they will be severely punished. It has been suggested that it is for this reason there have been no official acts of war in cyberspace as all sides are probably relatively balanced in terms of capability, and therefore are able to do considerable harm to any opponent.
Information domination	There is often an imbalance between the amount of information available to different parties in a disputed situation. When one or more individual or organization has considerably more information than other parties to the dispute, it can be said that they are in a position of information domination. This allows them to use this information to their advantage. Information domination may be used either offensively or defensively.
Information leaking	The unauthorized release of information into the public domain from an individual or an organization.

Term	Definition
Information monopoly	The term monopoly refers to the fact that in certain situations there is only one supplier of a commodity or service. At one time there were many monopolies in the UK where the government owned the railways, the national airline, the electricity and gas supply etc. Information monopoly occurs when there is only one source of information available. Many organizations attempt to funnel the information they release through a single channel such as an authorized spokesperson and this can be viewed as an act of information monopoly. However, there are often information leakages which mean that unauthorized information becomes available despite the efforts of the organization to control it.
Information operations (IO)	A military term used to describe the actions taken to both attack and/or protect cyber systems from adversaries.
Information security	Information which is not in the public domain is considered to be the property of an owner. Such information is normally controlled as it is regarded as having value. In order for its value to be retained it is important that it should not be readily available to the general public. Information security describes this attitude towards information as well as the activities which are required in order to ensure its protection from being released without authorization.
Information superiority	Individuals and organizations achieve information superiority when they have better access to information than a competitor and when they are in a position to use that information to obtain some advantage.

Term	Definition
Information terrorism	How the threat of the release of certain information could create fear or anxiety in a way similar to how people and organizations respond to the threat of real physical terrorism.
Information transparency	Information is transparent when it is open, understandable and clear. Another condition for information transparency is that it has to be obvious how the information has been obtained, and be able to demonstrate that every effort has been made to ensure its integrity.
Information warfare	The use of information to attack an opponent. The term information warfare is more general than cyber warfare as it includes traditional press releases, radio and television interviews, and any other means of disseminating information which can be disadvantageous to an individual, organization or nation state.
Infrastructure attacks	These are attacks on the basic assets of an organization or a nation.
	An attack on the data backup arrangements of an organization could be interpreted as an infrastructure attack, as could the overloading of the network which results in a denial of service situation.
	The recent attacks on the National Health System in the UK can be seen as an infrastructure attack on the nation.
Insider misuse	Insider misuse occurs when those who are employed by an organization or a nation state cause harm or inappropriately take advantage of the computer systems. This can happen in a number of ways including exposing or leaking information that should not have been exposed,

Term	Definition
	and can be accidental in some cases. Insider misuse is one of the biggest weaknesses of all organizations, as sometimes the people inside do not know they have exposed something important.
Insider threat	A threat that comes from within an organization or a nation state. Many cyber threats arise because of insiders who may accidently or purposefully damage a computer or network. The ability of insiders to do this is sometimes referred to as the weakest link in cyber security.
Instagram	A mobile, desktop, and Internet photo-sharing application and service that allows users to share pictures and videos either publicly or privately, to pre-approved followers.
Intellectual property law	Legislation protecting the rights of the owners of intangible assets such as ideas expressed in software, symbols, written material, music, visual arts etc.
Intelligence	In a number of communities, especially the military and law and order the word intelligence is used in the same sense as information. A formal description of military intelligence is a discipline which addresses the collection, analysis and use of information which can be used to advise commanders to make better decisions. *See Information.*
Intelligence based warfare	Active conflict that is informed by and conducted through the acquisition and analysis of appropriate information.

Term	Definition
International Information Systems Security Certification Consortium (ISC)[2]	A not-for-profit organization that provides security training and certification courses for cyber security professionals in the USA.
International law	The body of rules customs and treaties which have been established over many years to inform the ways in which nation states interact with one another. The purpose of international law is to provide good governance which will advance economic and social development as well as peace and security among nations. It incorporates a number of declarations such as the United Nations Declaration on Human Rights. Different countries subscribe to varying extents to the notion of international law and in general it has been difficult to implement.
Internet Governance Forum (IGF)	The Internet Governance Forum (IGF) brings together various stakeholders to discuss public policy issues relating to the Internet. The IGF facilitates a common understanding of the benefits and the challenges of the Internet.
Internet of Things (IoT)	The use of the Internet to connect devices such as motor vehicles, domestic appliances and ATMs to mention only a few. There is enormous potential to connect devices through the Internet, many of which are being currently exploited. For example by the cyberfication of homes where everything from fridges to cookers to boilers to doorbells are being connected to the Internet.

Term	Definition
Internet policy	Internet policy exists at several different and distinct levels. Firstly, there is Internet policy at the national level which refers to society's needs for high speed telecommunication connections. This may include both the laying of cabling throughout the country as well as the availability of WiFi hotspots. Internet policy also relates to how service providers behave with regards to pricing policies and various levels of protection to vulnerable individuals in the society. In addition to these national issues each organization will have an Internet policy with regards to which members of staff will have access to the Internet and what they are entitled to use this Internet for. For example, many organizations restrict their employees from using the corporate Internet for personal purposes. A comprehensive corporate Internet policy will address acceptable use; backup arrangements; confidentiality; mobile devices; passwords; physical security. It is also possible to have a personal Internet policy with regards to the age at which children are given mobile phones and the circumstances under which they are permitted to use them.
Internet Protocol (IP)	The rules by which data is transmitted across the Internet. *See IP Address.*
Internet transparency	The word transparency is used in a number of different ways and different contexts. This term is normally used to describe how the internet functions seamlessly without the need for any user to know how the data or voice or pictures

Term	Definition
	are transmitted across cyberspace. Another issue which falls under the heading of Internet transparency is the degree to which Internet facilities providers fully inform users as to the extent to which their digital footprint will be commercialized.
Internet watch foundation	A body set up in the UK to monitor content on websites. The objective is to make the internet safer, especially by the removal of images of child sexual abuse.
Intrusion detection systems	Security arrangements which are intended to detect unauthorized access to a computer or network.
Intrusion prevention system	Security arrangements which are intended to stop unauthorized access to a computer or network.
IP address	Each computer on the internet has at least one unique IP address which identifies it from all other computers on the Internet.

J

Journey mapping to Just war theory

Term	Definition
Joint operations	A mission or collection of missions undertaken by two or more agencies or countries working together for a common goal.
Journey mapping	*See Mission mapping.*
Jurisdiction	The legal area or district in which a crime has been committed and in which it may be prosecuted in accordance with the law. In cyberspace the identification of the jurisdiction of a cyber attack can be difficult.
Just war theory	Just War Theory is concerned with establishing the legal and moral foundations by which nation states can be justified in going to war. Just war theory has 3 divisions, JUS AD BELLUM, JUS IN BELLUM, and JUS POST BEELLUM. JUS AD BELLUM is concerned with establishing the conditions related to entering into a just war. JUS IN BELLUM is concerned with establishing the conditions related to the just conduct of war. JUS POST BELLUM is concerned with the moral issues related to the termination stage of war.

K

Killswitch to Knime analysis

Term	Definition
Killswitch	A single mechanism for shutting off any device. It is sometimes referred to as an emergency termination procedure.
Kinetic warfare	Military action involving active warfare. Cyber warfare is often described as non-kinetic warfare.
Knime analysis	An analytic platform to provide data driven innovative solutions.

L

Leak to Lulzec

Term	Definition
Leak	The release of information to the media which has not been authorized by an organization or an individual is described as a leak. It is the intentional disclosure of information which the organization or individual regards as confidential. It is regarded as a violation of trust and within the government context it can be a criminal act. Data or information acquired through the use of eavesdropping equipment has also been referred to as a leak from the organization.
Leeming, Cal	Cal Leeming is the youngest person to be convicted of hacking in the UK at the age of 12 years. Several years later he was convicted again of hacking and 11 counts of fraud amounting to £750,000. He was sentenced to 15 months in prison. He is now a security advisor and systems architect in Silicon Valley.
Linkedin	A business, professional and employment orientated social media website. The objective of this website is primarily related to employment opportunities and other professional activities including networking.
Logic bomb	Computer code which has been secretly inserted in a program or operating system which will be triggered to damage the computer or network when a particular event takes place. The event

Term	Definition
	could be a date or a number of transactions or some other item specified in the program code.
Lottery scam	A scam which has been designed around a false claim that an individual has won a prize in a lottery. Typically, this scam announces a large win and then informs the target that he or she will have to pay a processing fee in order to get access to their winnings. There is of course no lottery and thus no winnings and the fraudster absconds with the processing fee.
Lulzsec	A hacktivist group responsible for high profile attacks on several organizations including Sony Pictures, Nintendo, as well as the USA government. Lulzsec originally operated under the idea of "just for the lulz" meaning just for the laughs, but eventually branched out to have ideological motivations, such as preventing censorship and corruption in later attacks.

M

Machine learning to Multiple identities

Term	Definition
Machine learning	The ability of computer software to acquire the facility of being able to improve its performance through the recording of previous experience. Machine learning closely imitates how humans learn from mistakes. It is one aspect of artificial intelligence in which there has been much progress in recent years and which has allowed the development of significantly smarter machines.
Machine translation	Using technology to translate one language into another. Google has one of the best known machine translators which operate on a text to text basis. However, there are now also mobile voice language translators.
Mainstream media	The term is usually used to indicate where the political and business establishments first look for news. In the UK this includes the Times, the Telegraph, the Guardian newspapers as well as the BBC and ITV. In the USA mainstream media includes the Washington Post and the New York Times, USA Today, the Los Angeles Times newspapers and NBC and CNN TV stations. It would not include Algeciras or RT.
Malvertising	Computer advertising which will contaminate a computer with malware.
Malware	A term which covers the full range of software which has been designed to do harm to comput-

Term	Definition
	er systems and networks. It is often used as a synonym for computer viruses but it is actually a much broader concept.
Man in the browser attack	A Trojan horse type attack where the attacker intercedes between two parties and unbeknownst to the two parties the man in the middle conveys faulty information or possibly alters the information communicated between two parties while they continue to believe that they are in direct communication with one another.
Man in the middle attack	This type of attack involves the interruption of the flow of data without the sender of receiver being aware of it. The attacker locates him/herself in between these two nodes and therefore has access to the data flowing between them.
Manning, Chelsey (Bradley)	Private First Class Bradley Manning now Ms Chelsey Manning leaked to WikiLeaks classified documents on USA military actions and failures. Some of the information the leaks revealed were occasions of friendly fire in Bagdad and information on the deaths of civilians. He received a 35 year prison sentence (commuted to 7 years). After he was sentenced Bradley announced that he wanted to live as a woman and take the name of Chelsey Manning.
Mass marketing fraud	Large scale attempts to defraud targets through the use of intensive emailing. Phishing attacks are regarding as mass marketing fraud events. The number of targets in a single phishing attack is not known but it is expected that it is probably hundreds of thousands if not millions.

Term	Definition
Mass surveillance	The ability of any entity to listen in to verbal conversations or read written exchanges which are facilitated by Internet technology.
Memes	A soundbite in the form of an image, video or piece of text spread rapidly through the internet and which can morph as it is passed around.
Memory protection	A computer function which attempts to ensure that the memory of the computer is not inappropriately accessed.
Metadata	The prefix meta is derived from the Greek word meaning beyond and when used in the sense of meta it refers to a data set which contains information about other data. It is used in web content code as keywords that search engines will pick up.
Military intelligence	Information collected from any source and processed by military analysts in order to facilitate military decisions. *See Intelligence and Information.*
Misinformation	Mistaken information where the provider is unaware of the facts or the true state of affairs and is thus misinformed. In such cases the provider of this information may say, "I have misspoken". However, the term can also refer to fake news and fake data. In this instance misinformation is the presentation of incorrect, inaccurate or incomplete information as though it was authentic usually to support a particular agenda. Disinformation is a similar concept, but in this case the misinformer is aware of that they are disseminating untruths.

Term	Definition
Mission assurance	Actions performed to increase the probability that the mission will be a success. Mission assurance involves ongoing processes of assessment, monitoring and control.
Mission mapping	An expression of a mission plan which will normally be created visually or graphically in the form of a map showing the starting point and the end point of a mission and the various stages in between. Mission maps can be quite high level or they may contain much detail.
Mocking up	The combining of different images and texts normally found on the Internet in perfectly legitimate websites in order to create a new document.

When used maliciously mocking up is a way of creating a fake document such as an apparent notification from a bank or from a law enforcement agency in order to defraud or compromise an individual or organization.

Mocked up documents tend not to be perfect and may contain some sort of an error which can be detected by close examination of the fraudulent document. |
| **Modbus protocol** | Serial communication protocol commonly used in collecting industrial electronic equipment including Programmable Logic Controllers. |
| **Monetizing hacking** | In the early days of hacking computers were often attacked by individuals who wanted to demonstrate their expertise and their ability of being able to defeat the security arrangements in place. However, for some time now hacking has been largely monetized which means that hackers are looking for some way of improving their |

Term	Definition
	cash flow through their hacking activities. This can be accomplished by stealing IDs and PINs or it could be through blackmail and other forms of extortion.
Moore's law	A hypothesis put forward by Gordon Moore in the 1960s which asserted that the capacity of integrated circuits would double every year. Moore claimed that this phenomenon would last for at least a decade but in fact it has been far more sustainable than that.
Moving target defense strategy	In the arms race between the hackers and those who defend computers and networks there is continuous changing of approaches with the development of new malware, viruses and anti-virus software. The continual flow of new ideas and challenges may be seen as a moving target defense strategy. This is part of the arms race between the defenders and the attackers and is a strategy for protecting sensitive data that involves shifting the environment around the data on an interval basis instead of keeping it static.
Multiple identities	In order to reduce the probability of being detected and apprehended by law and order officials hackers tend to operate under a number of different names or identities. Multiple identities make it more difficult to know who is actually behind cyber attacks and therefore track them down.

N

National critical infrastructure to NSA spying programs

Term	Definition
National critical infrastructure	An infrastructure is comprised of the basic physical and organizational assets required for a system to function. The National Critical Infrastructure traditionally consists of roads and bridges, railways and canals, airports and harbors. Today the National Critical Infrastructure also consists of electricity and gas supply, telecommunications and radio connections and all other elements that underpin the efficient and effective operation of computers and networks. Some countries have defined National Infrastructure Sectors such as Chemicals, Civil Nuclear Communications, Defense, Emergency Services, Energy, Finance, Food, Government, Health, Space, Transport and Water etc.
Negative externalities	In economics a negative externality is a cost which is incurred by a third party when some economic activity takes place. The term can be used in other environments and a negative externality can be seen as a type of collateral damage which affects a third party when some particular action is taken.
Net neutrality	The concept of net neutrality suggests that governments should be impartial and that they should ensure that Internet providers treat all data exchanges over the Internet on an equal

Term	Definition
	basis. This does not mean that illegal data exchanges should go unchallenged.
New battle ground	Traditionally there was said to have been three battlegrounds which were on land where the army functioned, at sea which was the domain of the navy, and in the air where the airforce was the key player. Then it was said by some that Space, satellites etc. became the fourth battleground. However, there have been no known battles fought in space.

Today's new battleground is cyberspace.

In non-military terms cyberspace is the arena for conflict between those who wish to use the Internet for criminal or negative reasons and those who do not. As much as anything else this new battle ground is in the human mind. |
| **News feed** | A collection of news articles sent over the Internet, either chosen by the user or using an algorithm based on interest or preselection. |
| **Nigerian letter** | A form of fraud which predates the use of the Internet.

An invitation to participate in a nefarious activity usually involving a large sum of money whereby an individual is asked to assist in the collection of money from abroad. When the target responds to this invitation he/she is invited to send money to the fraudster who then most frequently disappears. On some occasions the fraudster will ask for money on several occasions or for as long as the victim is willing to pay.

The origins of this type of fraud can be traced |

Term	Definition
	back to the Middle Ages when it took the form of wealthy individuals being invited to participate in funding the repatriation of Spanish prisoners who were washed up in England when the Spanish Armada sank. Then the proposition was that the Spanish prisoner, who never really existed, was the son of a nobleman who would pay handsomely for his return to Spain.
Non-government cyber actor	Any individual or organization which is active across the Internet and which is not an agent of a government or a nation state.
Norms for cyberspace behavior	Behind the idea of establishing norms for cyberspace behavior is the fact that the Internet and the web have become so important to everyday existence at the personal, organizational and nation state level, that it has now become essential to establish agreement as to how it should be used and protected. One of the central issues here is that the Internet should be considered a neutral zone which is safeguarded against unwarranted intervention by national governments.
NSA spying programs	Surveillance programs initiated by the NSA in the name of fighting global terrorism after the September 11, 2001 attacks on the USA. The program "Stellar Wind" was one of the first, with the goal of warrantless surveillance of American citizens through the collection of internet communications and activities. This program provided the legal framework which led to the creation of larger programs, including PRISM, MUSCULAR, and more. These newer programs absorb millions of records a day from organizations and from Internet lines.

O

Offensive cyber operation to Opt out

Term	Definition
Offensive cyber attack	A deliberate and perhaps unprovoked and un-wanted cyber intervention on a computer or network system.
Offensive Cyber Operation (OCO)	The execution of activities and resources re-quired to launch an offensive cyber attack.
OODA loop	The acronym OODA represents observe, orient, decide, and act.
	It is a decision cycle used by the USAF at the operational level during military campaigns. It is today used in a wide range of professional environments including, legal, business, law enforcement and of course the military.
Open access	Computer output which is available for all to use without permission and without paying a fee. There is the perception that the results of research are often restricted by the fact that they are published in expensive academic journals the subscriptions for which can run into hun-dreds or thousands of dollars. Open access is intended to make the findings of research avail-able to all. There is a growing body of work which is published through open access vehi-cles. Open access is not uncontroversial one of the issues being that it is costly to operate an open access journal and if the readers are not

Term	Definition
	paying these expenses then it becomes necessary to have the authors pay for the publication of the research findings. There has been resistance to this idea. There is a directory of open access journals at https://doaj.org/ Open access also refers to certain newspapers, books and other information on the Internet that is free to access.
Open source	This term mostly refers to software which is available to use without permission and without paying a fee. Open source software was created as a reaction to the high cost of purchasing the well known branded software products. The intention of open source is to make software products available quickly and to a large section of the public. Although free to acquire there may be costs associated with setting up open source systems and with maintaining them.
Open source intelligence (Osint)	Data collected from publicly available sources to be used in an intelligence context. In the intelligence community, the term "open" refers to overt, publicly available sources (as opposed to covert or clandestine sources). It is not related to open source software or public intelligence.
Operations security	In a general sense operations security involves ensuring that the functioning of a system or an entity can proceed without the likelihood of interruption. It involves processes that identify vulnerable aspects of the operation and develops plans to ensure that this vulnerability is reduced to a minimum. Operations security procedures need to be implemented, monitored and con-

Term	Definition
	trolled.
	Part of operations security is to identify if critical information can be observed by adversaries who might wish to do harm to the system. If such incidents are discovered then appropriate action needs to be taken.
Opt in	The process of declaring one's interest in participating in an event. The concept of opt in often applies to email lists. Some organizations create email lists as a result of an individual purchasing an item from them. When the purchase is made the purchaser is invited to opt in to receive further information from the organization. As a result of this the purchaser will be informed of new products and services on offer. It is generally considered that this is the most satisfactory way of creating and operating a marketing emailing list.
Opt out	Declaring that one is not interested in participating on an event. An opt out situation occurs when an individual is automatically included in an emailing list without specifically requesting this inclusion and has to request to be removed from the list. In many places this is no longer considered to be a satisfactory way of conducting business.

P

Passcode to Pyscho-demographic profile

Term	Definition
Passcode	A series of private and personal numbers required to access an account or a system on a computer or a network. The supplier of the system often sets Passcodes but there is usually a provision whereby the user can reset the pass code to numbers which are chosen by him or her.
Passwords	Privately established and secretively protected words or combinations of words and numbers and special characters which when entered into a cyber device allow the holder of the password to have access to the functionality of the system. Passwords are essential in establishing any level of security with regards to cyber devices and Internet systems. However, passwords are often seen as an annoyance by the user and are not always given appropriate attention.
Penetration testing	The term penetration testing normally refers to assessing the robustness of cyber defenses. Thus it is the act of conducting a simulated cyber attack on a network or system to test for possible vulnerabilities. The testing is usually conducted by a specialized outside organization using a variety of skills including social engineering and cyber knowledge.

Term	Definition
Personal Identification Number (PIN)	Personal Identification Number or PIN operates in much the same way as a password but it is by its nature strictly numeric. PINs are now required to access an increasingly large range of services. They are often part of two-stage security and used together with a password.
Personality profiling	The use of data to create a relatively abstract model of an individual and their likely behavior. In cyberspace a personality profile is typically created using data from either social media or from products such as Google in order to anticipate the behavior, traditionally purchasing behavior, of individuals. Personality profiling has become more controversial recently with the disclosure that political parties and others have used it in attempting to influence the outcome of elections. This has become a major issue in both the USA and in the UK through the activities of Cambridge Analytica. However, it has not yet been established that the interventions made during the 2016 presidential election in the USA or the Brexit referendum had any actual effect on the outcome.
Phishing	Phishing is a cyber attack usually aimed at a target whereby the attacker informs the individual that his or her account has been compromised and that in order to correct the situation it is necessary for the target to reveal personal details including bank account details, ID, and passwords. These personnel details are then used in a form of identity theft to steal money or other resources from the target. A variant of the phishing scam is where the computer user receives a call claiming to come from an Internet supplier or some other respectable cyber vendor

Term	Definition
	which says that an error has been identified on their system and that for a fee paid right away this problem can be corrected. There is of course no problem on the system and the target is simply relieved of his or her money.
Phony terminals	Devices used by fraudsters to acquire ID and PIN numbers. In some cases fraudsters have actually built fake devices which are identical in appearance to legitimate ATMs but whose sole purpose is to record credit card numbers, IDs and PIN of unsuspecting users. These fake ATMs do not dispense money but will capture the details of the unsuspecting public.
Physical infrastructure	Physical infrastructure is a wide-ranging con-cept which can include buildings and furniture as well as electricity supply, WiFi access etc. *See Critical national infrastructure.*
Physical security	Physical security can take many forms ranging from armed guards with or without dogs to guard gates and fences with or without barbed wire. In normal circumstances physical security often amounts to the keeping safe of property including software and data by ensuring that it is under lock and key while not in use. More recently biometrics, using fingerprints, voice recognition and iris scanning can be seen as forms of physical security.
PIN entry device	A terminal such as a handheld card reader or an ATM machine. These devices test whether the PIN that is entered is valid. This test is executed by the device looking up the PIN from where it is stored either on a magnetic strip or on a mi-crochip on a plastic card.

Term	Definition
Piracy	This term originally referred to acts of criminal violence committed at sea or in coastal areas. It often involves both theft and murder. This type of piracy has existed from ancient times but was particularly active in the late mediaeval and early modern ages. Although the word is still used in this sense today, with there being considerable piracy activity in certain areas of the world especially around the Horn of Africa, it has been extended to refer to the use of cyber assets, primarily software, which has not been purchased through legitimate channels. In the cyberspace context piracy is considered as a euphemism for theft.
Platform	A term to describe a group of technologies employed to deliver a solution or service. Thus the i-Phone may be said to work on an Apple platform, whereas other mobile phones use the Android platform.
	Then there are systems that offer a facility for users to upload data (also referred to as content) of their choice to a platform. Thus Facebook has been described as a platform where individuals upload personal information about themselves as well as about their activities. The essence of this type of platform is that its owners insist that they are not responsible for the content which users upload to the platform. This notion is currently being challenged as there are strong objections from the public and from governments about the fact that some platforms have been used to disseminate objectionable material which in some cases includes hate messages. It has even been pointed out that these platforms may be used to facilitate and access material

Term	Definition
	related to terrorism. Platform owners are beginning to take more notice of the views of governments, which are threatening to take action against them if they do not change their attitude to the monitoring of the content placed on the platforms.
Point of Sale Intrusions	A cyber attack on a point of sale device such as a terminal within a supermarket, or electronic vending machines etc.
Police scam	A scam whereby the target is informed that he or she has committed some sort of offence and that a fine has to be paid. This scam will be communicated to the target on a fraudulent or mocked up document which purports to be from a police agency or department. Such documents are particularly frightening to either inexperienced individuals or to those who are elderly, and as a result these groups are regularly targeted with this scam.
Post truth	A term which has been coined to describe the current era in which it has been said there has been a large increase in fake news. However, it is not at all clear that there has been a significant increase in the distortion of news. False news is a long-term phenomenon dating back to ancient times, which has been highlighted by the discourse of the 2016 Presidential election in the USA. But as fake news or false news has been identified in Roman times its roots stem far back in history.
	In modern times the Blair government in the UK was famous for putting a spin on information they released in order to present their achievements in the best possible light. In a

Term	Definition
	sense this is no different from fake news.
	The term post truth has been used by political establishments whose intentions were overturned. For example, after the 2016 Presidential election in the USA or by the outcome of the Brexit referendum. The term post truth is best used with ironical intentions and employed as a trigger for discussion rather than a statement of fact.
Postmodern warfare	The term postmodern is used in a number of different ways but with regards to warfare, the suggestion here is that we have moved beyond fighting with traditional weapons which are designed to physically destroy people and property. Using this point of view postmodern warfare is really a synonym for cyber warfare whereby considerable damage may be done to individuals and to society without causing kinetic or bodily harm to anyone and without the destruction of physical property. Of course, cyber warfare involves the destruction of intangible property such as data and software, and it can also result in the wellbeing of individuals being seriously damaged.
Prism	The name of a USA National Security Agency (NSA) program which collects internet communications from various USA internet companies. This program was brought to the attention of the public as a result of the Edward Snowden revelations.
Privacy	The notion that individuals in particular, but also other entities, have the right to prevent public access to information about their life and deeds. This is a complex issue as the boundaries

Term	Definition
	around what is considered private information differs from culture to culture, and between individuals within the same culture.
	Privacy is an integral part of national and corporate policy which has been under pressure from the innovations created by cyber developments. Social software like Facebook invites its members to provide personal information which a few years ago would have been considered by many to be an invasion of their privacy. Furthermore, a number of different web applications behave in a similar way, collecting data about those who use them which is also considered to be an invasion of privacy. A primary example is the issue of personality profiling by organizations for marketing purposes. Through the data offered by individual members of Facebook, together with their indications of *likes* and *dislikes*, machine learning programs can develop personality profiles which may be used for targeted marketing.
	Ultimately privacy is about being able to control information about your own personal life, and not to have other individuals comment on your preferences or indeed your performance.
Privacy campaigners	Individuals who feel strongly that their ability to conduct their lives outside of the purview of the public and who are prepared to take some action can sometimes become privacy campaigners. Privacy campaigners object to the proliferation of video cameras in public places, and the propensity of social media platforms and web browsers to record their activities on the Internet.

Term	Definition
Privacy settings	Many software products allow administrators to configure their functionality so that users are to a greater or lesser extent in control of what is being recorded by the software, and what is being passed onto it owners. This of course varies considerably from one software product to another. This functions through the manipulation of privacy settings within the particular system being used.
Privilege management	The functionality of a piece of software is often described as consisting of a series of privileges. The most basic functions of the software would be considered to be the privileges awarded to any user of a system. Other more advanced and perhaps more useful aspects of the software could be controlled by the administrator and only released to individuals who had a clear need to access these functionalities. The control of these aspects of the system is sometimes referred to as privilege management and can form an important part of a security strategy.
Profiling	A form of data analysis which allows for the hypothesizing of personalized behavioral characteristics of an individual. In general terms a profiler looks at the record of activities undertaken by an individual and attempts to use this data to arrive at an understanding of how the individual thinks and what type of behavior could be expected from him or her in the future. Profiling has been used by law and order agencies in their attempts to apprehend criminals. In recent years it has been used for marketing purposes, but now the attention of profiling has been switched to the political arena.

Term	Definition
Propaganda	Any statement which focuses on delivering an unbalanced message and which deliberately ignores any other point of view. However, the term is normally associated with periods of conflict especially those of warfare where each side attempts to exaggerate accounts of their successes and minimize any description of their losses. The essence of propaganda is that it is a highly biased account of the situation and its verisimilitude should be questioned.
Proportional response	When an act of aggression has been experienced by a nation state or an organization, it is often thought appropriate that an act of retaliation is performed. The question then arises as to how severe such a retaliatory action should be. A proportional response is a retaliatory act which does approximately the same amount of harm to the aggressor as the aggressor did in the first act of hostility.
Protect IP Act (PIPA)	A law proposed in the USA, PIPA is known as the "Prevent Real Online Threats to Economic Creativity and Theft of Intellectual Property Act". This bill was supposed to help curb copyright infringement, but the proposed method to enforce it was subject to pushback by individuals and corporations. The proposed law would allow the removal of deemed "rouge websites" from the DNS, effectively blacklisting the site unless the individual knew the IP address of the website. The concern was who defined what "a rouge website" was and the potential for misuse was of grave concern. As of 2018, the bill has not been returned for debate or a vote.

Term	Definition
Psychological profiling	*See Personality profiling.*
Psychological warfare	Nonviolent conflict between individuals, organizations or nation states. The essence of psychological warfare is that opponents attempt to either belittle each other or maximize the importance of their own achievements and exaggerate the absence of achievements in the other party. Psychological warfare uses psychological operations (Psyops) and employs techniques of social engineering. At a personal level psychological warfare can be described as one-upmanship, but in the organizational or nation state arena it can be much more damaging.
Psyops	A military term used to describe the selection and distribution of information to a select group of individuals in order to influence or alter their emotions, behavior, or motives based on a desired outcome. The name suggests secret manipulation including the use of propaganda. Activities such as dropping leaflets from aircraft radio broadcasts, loudspeaker vans have at some time come under the heading of psyops.
Public core of the internet	The sum of the essential protocols and infrastructure required for the Internet to function. These key protocols and infrastructure can be considered to be a global public good that provides benefits to everyone in the world.
Public intelligence	In the military sense the term intelligence has the same meaning as information in the non-military environment. Therefore, public intelligence is the way the military describes information known to the public, i.e., in the public domain.

Term	Definition
Public open WiFi hot spots	Areas where free WiFi is offered to the public such as in restaurants, hotels, buses etc. WiFi offered in these areas is often provided free of charge and is relatively unprotected. This source of a WiFi connection is normally thought to be insecure.
Pyscho-demographic profile	An account of the psychological and personal characteristics of an individual. This type of profiling is performed in order to understand consumer behavior as well as to assist in criminal investigations. Recently pyscho-demographic profiling has been applied in the political arena to elections and referenda.

Ransomware to Russian doctrine of information security

Term	Definition
Ransomware	A piece of malware which is introduced to a computer or network in order to retard, disrupt or prevent its operation. Once the system has been affected the originators of this attack will inform the owners that if a sum of money (ransom) is paid, the malware will be removed or neutralized. There have been a number of high profile cyber ransom cases in recent years including one affecting a number of NHS hospitals in the UK. In the USA the Medstar hospital attack is another prime example. The cyber attack on Sony pictures was also a cyber ransom demand.
Reactive cyber security	An approach to protecting cyber assets which have been affected by a cyber attack by eliminating the points of weakness revealed and implementing procedures to ensure that they do not reoccur.
Red alert	A strong indication that there is a problem or a potential problem. As net neutrality is coming under pressure in the USA an increasing number of websites are posting red alerts. The purpose of the red alert is to draw attention to a change in the way the website may operate in the future.

Term	Definition
Red flag	When an attack has been detected or when the vulnerability becomes apparent, the computer or network system may raise a red flag to draw attention to the situation.
Red team	In simulation exercises designed to test cyber resilience the team of individuals who are required to attack the computer system or network are often referred to as the *red team*.
Reddit	Established in 2005 Reddit is an American social news aggregation website predominantly aimed at users who desire to share links, photos, stories, and other information. Known for its Subreddits (communities centered around a particular topic within Reddit) the website claims to have thousands of such communities.
Remote access	Remote access allows a user to log into a system as an authorized user without actually being present at the same site as the computer. This was traditionally undertaken through a terminal but today it can be from any digital device, mobile or otherwise, that has appropriate communications facilities.
Removable device	A memory stick, disk drive, SD card or a CD. It is any device that can be plugged into and easily removed from a cyber device.
Removing Google content	Internet users may request that content should be removed from Google. This is achieved by completing an online form. It should not be assumed that the content no longer exists in Google's backup systems.
Retweet	Term used to describe the resending of messages received in Twitter.

Term	Definition
Revenge porn	The distribution of intimate video or photographs by an estranged lover in order to take revenge by embarrassing the target/victim. Depending on the material uploaded to the web or distributed by email revenge porn may or may not be illegal. However, it normally creates a high degree of psychological distress in the victim.
Right to privacy	There is today considerable controversy over this issue. In the past it was generally felt that everyone had a right to privacy. However, in recent years this attitude has begun to change and it is now argued that those who put themselves into the public eye are in affect giving up their rights of privacy. This means that in the case of individuals in the public eye their activities are suitable to be commented on by the media, both traditional and alternative.
Risk	The risk of an event is the probability that the expected results will not be achieved. There are many different types of risks some of which are knowable and some are unknowable and risks can also be manageable or unmanageable. There are risks which could have a major impact on a situation and risks which will only result in minor inconvenience. A significant element of cyber security is the identification, assessment and management of risk which allows resources to be focused on issues that are really important.
Romance scam	This is a well known cyber attack on an individual whereby a person establishes a connection (i.e. becomes a cyber friend) and appears to have a personal relationship with the target, usually using email or a social media platform.

Term	Definition
	The target comes to believe that the relationship is based on a deep emotional attraction and that person then becomes the victim of a fraud.
	In this scam the cyber friend usually asks for the loan of money to pay for some sort of emergency while promising that it will be repaid. Sometimes once the money is received the cyber friend will disappear. On other occasions the cyber friend will continue to ask for money over a period of multiple months or even years. Once the target is no longer prepared to supply the funds the fraudster closes the connection and disappears.
Rouge website	This term was used in the PIPA debate in the USA. A rouge website is one which purports to be something which it is not.
	Websites can be created which appear to be from a particular commercial organization such as a bank, and when the user attempts to use the website his or her personal details are stolen for the purposes of identity theft.
Russian doctrine of information security	Document addressing national information security policy approved in 2016 by the Russian President which outlines the views of the Russian Federation for Information Security within that country. It states that this doctrine is needed because of "The scale of special services of individual states using means of information and psychological impact aiming to destabilize intra-political and social situation in different parts of the world ... is expanding."

S

Term	Definition
SCADA (Supervisory Control and Data Acquisition)	A cyber system comprising hardware and software which facilitates industrial control. It can collect data in real time from remote locations. It is used power plants as well as in oil and gas refining, telecommunications, transportation, and water and waste control.
Scam	An act of illegally extracting money from a non-discerning individual. It is a form of fraud in which an individual is offered a product or service which is "too good to be true". Scamming is an old activity and its roots can be traced into antiquity. Scams can also be perpetrated against organizations.
Scammer	An individual who attempts or actually perpetrates a scam. These are individuals who are attempting or actually committing a fraud.
Scope of attack	An attack on a target can be highly focused to the point of addressing a minuscule target such as a vehicle or a small building. On the other hand, attacks can be far more general, an example of which is that of carpet bombing, where the intention is to destroy large surface areas held by the enemy. The scope of the attack describes the position taken by the attacker along the spectrum between being highly focused and being the cyber equivalent of carpet bombing.

Term	Definition
Script kiddies	Individuals who use already established malware to attack cyber targets. The suggestion is that these individuals are not yet adequately mature to be able to write their own malware code to do this task.
Secure code execution	Cyberspace can only function because vendors of hardware, software etc. are trusted to deliver products which do not harbor nefarious code designed to do harm. Secure code execution is code supplied by the market which is executed by a system and is deemed trustworthy at all levels, i.e. usually based on secure keys or certificates.
Secure drop	An open source software platform which facilitates secure communications between journalists and their informants. It is intended to offer some confidence to whistleblowers that they can remain anonymous.
Security	A state in which a person, an organization or a nation state are free of potential harm or attack.
Security by design	When security arrangements are conceived as a fundamental part of a system and not simply something that has subsequently been added on as an afterthought. *See Security engineering.*
Security engineering	In the complex environment in which we operate in the 21st century, security cannot be taken for granted. The default assumption is that all systems are vulnerable to attack, and, that there is a high or even very high probability that all systems will eventually be attacked. In order to minimize the probability of an attack and to reduce the impact of any attack, it is essential that

Term	Definition
	careful planning be put in place at the earliest possible date. The process of identifying the potential attacks and the likelihood of these happening, i.e., identifying the risks involved, the preparation of plans, and the execution of these plans together with their monitoring and updating can be referred to as security engineering.
Seeders	Individuals who volunteer their personal data to be used as input to psychological profiling, which can then be used in computer-based personality judgment systems.
Self signed certificates	In cyberspace, a self-signed certificate is an identity certificate that is signed by the same entity whose identity it certifies. A self-signed certificate is one validated with its own private key.
Seleznev, Roman	Roman Seleznev also known as Track2 is a Russian high visibility hacker who was indicted in the USA in 2011.
Semantic attacks	An attack in which a computer record or the content of a website is changed, but in such a way that it does not appear to have been altered. The change has been affected in order to deliver a situation in which the information might be accepted as genuine by whoever reads the record or looks at the website.
Sexting	The sending and receiving a sexually explicit text, images or photographs via text messages.
Sextortion	A wide-ranging term which includes extracting money from a target who has been enticed into some sort of sexual activity on the Internet.

Term	Definition
Silk road	A dark web trading website which was closed down by the Government of the USA. The owner/initiator of this website was imprisoned for life with no option for parole.
Simulated malware	The activity of exploring the effect of a malware attack. The term simulated malware is also used to describe a system used to either test malware or to investigate the effect of a malware attack.
Simulation	A simulation is a life-like enactment/creation of a situation. It involves the ability to create, for the purposes of training or research, a situation which has all or many of the characteristics of a real environment in order to learn from a controlled life-like experience/experiment. It is now regarded as good practice to simulate cyber attacks in order to ensure that the cyber defenses of a system are adequate and that it will not be damaged or only minimally damaged by cyber attack. Highly skilled individuals will often engage in ethical (or white hat) hacking simulations for this purpose.
Snapchat	Multimedia messaging app released in 2011 focusing on photos.
Snowden, Edward	An American computer professional who was a Central Intelligence Agency employee and who leaked classified information from the National Security Agency in 2013. He disclosed the existence of a number of secret global surveillance programs. He was condemned by a number of government and law enforcement agencies in the USA. He is wanted by the USA authorities on various charges related to treason. He is currently resides in Russia.

Term	Definition
Social engineering cyber attack	The use of psychology to create a situation in which the behavior of a computer user opens up a vulnerability. The dropping of a USB drive in a public place for an unknowing individual to pick up is a classic social engineering cyber attack.
Social media	Websites and applications which facilitate the creation and sharing of personal data by users. The popularity of social media software has been exceptional and was not originally anticipated. Facebook alone claims more than 2 billion registered users.
Social media warfare	Using social media platforms as a cyber weapon. *See Google Scholar.*
Software Defined Radio (SDR)	A radio communication system in which physical components are implemented by means of executing software on a personal computer or some similar cyber device.
Sony pictures	The object of a particularly large scale cyber attack on 24 November 2014, where the corporation was held to ransom if it did not restrict the release of the film which portrayed the leader of North Korea in a way which was offensive to the North Koreans. Sony pictures refused to do this and the hackers made available to the public a large quantity of confidential information about Sony pictures.
Source of the Crime	This term can refer to the individuals who initiated a cyber attack, or it can refer to the country or jurisdiction from which a cyber attack was launched. In cyberspace the source of a criminal cyber attack may not be obvious as there are

Term	Definition
	various methods by which cyber criminals can obscure the origin of the attack. Such attempts to cover the attribution of a cyber attack are known as anti-forensics.
Spam	An email sent by a person or organization to someone not personally known to them which is unwanted and unwelcome by its recipient. Spam usually consists of advertising material, but it may also contain viruses and other malware. Carefully targeted spam email is usually how criminal cyber attacks such as phishing are delivered.
Spanish Prisoner scam	*See the Nigerian Letter scam*
Spearphishing cyber attack	Also known as an email spoofing attack, a spearphishing cyber attack is aimed specifically at one individual in the hope of ensnaring them in some way. This is normally by attempting to obtain specific personal confidential information which can be used to defraud them of funds. Phishing attacks are similar to spearphishing attacks, but are more general in nature, because a spearfishing cyber attack is focused on a particular individual.
Specialist cybercrime unit	In various parts of the world cybercrime is sufficiently prevalent that specialized police units have been set up in order to handle criminal incidents, as well as to attempt to educate the public, so that they become less likely to be victims of this type of crime.
Speed of attack	In cyber warfare this is the time required from the development of an attack concept to the actual initiation of the attack itself.

Term	Definition
Spoofing	In cyberspace the nearest synonym for spoofing is imitating or masquerading. In a phishing attack the fraudster often pretends to be a bank and thus this type of attack may be referred to as a spoof attack.
Spyware	Software which allows the surreptitious monitoring of computer systems, especially with regards to system usage. Spyware is often used by an organization in order to monitor the type of activities which their employees undertake when using their computers.
SSH remote attacks	SSH is an acronym for Secure Shell and provides a way of executing commands, making changes, and configuring services remotely. A SSH Remote Attack is well-known and popular form of attack on a network server. It is also known as a brute force attack.
Standard procedures	The way activities are designated to be conducted in an organization. In the cyber environment there will be standard procedures with regards to who is entitled to use the various applications in the organization, including email, websites etc., and which computers users will be allowed to log-in to. There will often be procedures with regards the use of mobile telephones as well as removable devices such as memory sticks and CDs. Standard procedures are an important element of any cyber security policy.
State control	The extent to which the state or the government should control the Internet and the web has become an important issue and has given rise to a considerable amount of debate in the UK and to potential legislation in the USA. In other less democratic countries there is a significant

Term	Definition
	amount of state control over which websites can be accessed and what can be said using the Internet. In Western countries there is relatively little state control, except where illegal activities are concerned. In addition, there are those who argue that because cyberspace has become so critically important in the lives of individuals and organizations, as well as in the operation of the day-to-day functioning of a nation state, it should be brought under centralized state control.
	Because cyberspace exists beyond national boundaries it is not easy to see how this could be effected. International treaties would be required and the process of acquiring these is fraught with difficulty. Even if national treaties were in place, there is then the issue of how these treaties would be enforced and how action could be taken against defaulters.
	In general state control is not seen as a desirable option.
State cyber actor	An employee or agency which is engaged in the cyber domain often for the purposes of improving security arrangements at the national level. It is taken for granted that a State cyber actor for a hostile nation could be interested in finding vulnerabilities in the cyber security arrangements of an adversary.
Stop online piracy act (SOPA)	There has been great concern in the USA about the potential of the Internet and the web to support the illegal distribution of copyrighted material. This concern has resulted in several attempts to pass legislation which will give the state powers to close down rogue websites as

Term	Definition
	well as take action against anyone who is deemed to be engaging in any form of software or data piracy. However, there has been considerable backlash against the possibility of this type of legislation being passed by Congress. A number of the most important players on the web have petitioned against SOPA as well as the Protect IP Act (PIPA) and at this point efforts to enact this type of legislation have stalled.
Street cashier	An individual who plays a role at street level in a cyber attack on ATMs. They use fraudulently acquired PINs to collect the cash the bank machines.
Structured cyber asymmetry	Asymmetry suggests lack of balance. In cyberspace an asymmetric attack is one whereby one individual can attack and do serious harm to a whole organization and maybe even a nation state. Structured cyber asymmetry describes how it is possible for one individual or perhaps a small group of individuals to cause as much damage to a target that would have required a large team of people only a few years ago.
Stuxnet	A malicious virus in the form of a worm first identified when it attacked the Iranian Nuclear Program. Although uncovered in 2010 it is thought to have been developed as early as 2005. Sources differ but some say that Stuxnet set the Iranian Nuclear Program back by several years. It has been suggested that this worm was developed by USA and Israeli computer scientists.

Term	Definition
Suckers list	A term used to describe a list of names of individuals who are likely to succumb to the temptation offered by criminals. Once an individual has been defrauded his or her name is often distributed to other fraudsters in the expectation that if they succumbed to one fraud they are more likely to fall for another.
Surface internet	The normal Internet used by most people and organizations, as opposed to the deep web and the dark web. Websites on the surface Internet are indexed by all the major search engines.
Surgical cyber-strikes	A highly targeted and precise cyber attack which is aimed at a specific individual or a particular class of individual.
System/ network breach	Similar to data breach but focused on the cyber devices within a system and within a network. The objective of a system breach could be to obtain data or it could be to damage some of the components of the computer or the network. *See data breach.*
System/ network hardening	The reduction of the opportunities to attack a system or network. The purpose of this is to reduce the risk of attack.

T

Tails to Twitter storm

Term	Definition
Tails	Tails stands for The Amnesic Incognito Live System and it is an operating system released in 2009 that aims at preserving anonymity. It is associated with TOR. This operating system is designed to be used from a CD or a USB
Tallinn manual	A comprehensive account of how existing international law applies in cyberspace. The second edition was published in 2013. The production of the manual was facilitated by the NATO Cooperative Cyber Defense Centre of Excellence.
Tamper proof terminals	It has been suggested by the banks that remote point-of-sale devices and ATMs are tamperproof. However, this is a controversial claim as there is much evidence to contradict this assertion.
Target	The object of a cyber attack which may range from defrauding an individual, to attempting to destroy a nuclear power station, to compromising the trust of a democratic nation in its voting system. The target is where the damage of the attack is intended to be felt.
The 3 Cs of Security Awareness	The 3 Cs of Security Awareness is a way of talking about possible action to prevent cyber attacks in the future. There are a number of different interpretations of what the Cs stand for which include Communications, Collaborations,

Term	Definition
	and Culture. Other sources referred to the three Cs as Cyber Information Sharing, Cloud computing and Cognitive computing.
The cloud	*See Cloud computing.*
The Pirate Bay	The Pirate Bay describes itself as, "… an online index of digital content of entertainment media and software. Founded in 2003 by Swedish think tank Piratbyrån, The Pirate Bay allows visitors to search, download, and contribute magnet links and torrent files, which facilitate peer-to-peer file sharing among users of the Bit Torrent protocol."
Tier one threat	A substantial threat to a nation state. In a number of countries cyber attacks are considered among the most dangerous threats which the country faces. In some incidences cyber threats are being discussed in the same terms as weapons of mass destruction. A tier one threat is one which a risk assessment has given great weight to as being likely to occur and which would inflict considerable damage.
TOR (The onion router)	A web access tool which improves user anonymity by defending them against traffic analysis. The technology behind TOR was originally developed by the USA Naval research laboratory in the 1990s but the first public release of the system was in 2004. TOR describes itself as "an effective censorship circumvention tool, allowing its users to reach otherwise blocked destinations or content. TOR can also be used as a building block for software developers to create new communication tools with built-in privacy features."

Term	Definition
Transparency	In cyberspace this term is used in much the same way as it is in everyday language and refers to the ability of something to be seen and therefore known. Something that is not transparent is hidden.
	There is an increasing demand for transparency in cyberspace especially with regards to how the data of individuals is being used by social media platforms for the purposes of marketing,
Trojan horse	A form of malware which is disguised and contained within legitimate software and which lays dormant until it is triggered by some event, after which it attacks the computer and/or network system in which it has been resident. There are a large number of possible triggers which may be used.
Troll	An individual who sends spiteful or hate messages through the Internet in order to offend or bully another individual. It is a highly repugnant form of antisocial behavior. It is illegal in some countries and can attract a jail sentence.
Troll farm	A group or an organization which creates and dispatches Troll messages.
	See Troll.
Trust but verify	A term made popular during the presidency of Ronald Reagan in the USA during his negotiations with Mikhail Gorbachev the leader of the USSR. The essence of the expression was that trust should not be given without there being clear evidence that it is well placed and that this evidence can only be acquired by inspection of the issues under discussion. Today the term is sometimes used with regards to the extent to

Term	Definition
	which cyber defenses should be regarded as not vulnerable.
Tumblr	Tumblr is a social media service with a focus on blogging and sharing of information. Tumblr is especially known for its ease-of-use with regards to photo blogs.
Tweet	Name given to a message created in Twitter. *See Retweet.*
Twitter	A social media platform introduced in 2006 for the exchange of short messages. It is the preferred medium of communication for the incumbent President of the USA and is an important element in what is regarded as alternative media. Twitter was originally confined to messages containing only 140 characters but this limit was doubled in 2017. Twitter is seen by many to be controversial in that it is claimed that much of the content of the message is spam, self-promotion or pointless babble.
Twitter storm	Rapid increase in the volume of Twitter traffic.

U

Unrecognized email to User behaviour analytics

Term	Definition
Unmanned aircraft system (UAS)	The combination of a remotely guided aerial vehicle (drone), a ground-based controller and a system of communication between the two.
Unmanned Aerial Vehicle (UAV)	Commonly known as a drone, a UAV is a remotely controlled aircraft without a pilot on board. It is the hardware component of a UAS.
Unrecognized email	The receipt of an email from an unknown source. There can be a high risk associated with opening an email from an unrecognized source and it is recommended that such emails be deleted rather than opened.
Unreported/under reported	In the commercial world cyber attacks are not always reported to the authorities because of the negative publicity associated with them.
User Behavior Analytics (UBA)	Tools available to facilitate psychological profiling using data retrieved from user logs. *See Psychological profiling.*

Virtual terrorism to Vulnerability protection

Term	Definition
Virtual terrorism	It is not easy to accurately define the image which is created by the use of the term virtual terrorism. In most instances the term virtual is being used as a synonym for cyber. Therefore, virtual terrorism is often a synonym for cyber terrorism. *See Cyber terrorism.*
Virtual war	In most instances the term virtual is being used as a synonym for cyber i.e. virtual war equals cyber warfare. On the other hand, the term virtual war could be used to describe a struggle which has produced a significant level of unpleasantness is not yet at a stage where it can be considered to be warfare. *See Cyber war.*
Virtualized networks	A network that has been decoupled from the normal underlying cyber assets of hardware and has been created in order to better integrate the functionality of the network into any group of hardware. It has also been described as the creation/simulation of network capability without the underlying network hardware.
Virus	A form of malware, a virus is computer code designed to interrupt the orderly operation of a computer system or a network of computer systems. Viruses can cause inconveniences or they

Term	Definition
	can be destructive to software and data. There is a wide range of these viruses or unwelcome computer code each of which has a separate strategy for doing harm to the computer or network. Viruses were originally spread by passing disks around but today they are usually transmitted across the internet.
Vulnerability	The degree to which an adversary can do damage or embarrass an individual, an organization or a nation state. It is a weakness in a computer or network system which can be exploited. The system can also be vulnerable to accidental damage.
Vulnerability protection	Vulnerability protection has become an important element in any cyber security policy. It consists of hardware, software and other physical and psychological devices or procedures which may be put in place to protect a system and thereby reduce or eliminate any vulnerability. This is primarily a question of having adequate cyber protection policies which are strictly implemented, monitored and enforced. There are many products on the market which claim to be able to do this.

War to Worm

Term	Definition
War	Traditionally a state of hostility between two or more nation states. A special case is the circumstances where civil order breaks down within a country and this is referred to as a Civil War. A war may be overt or covert. The Vietnamese war was an open or overt war whereas the hostilities between the USA and the USSR in the post 1945 period was a covert war which was also referred to as a Cold War. In recent years the term has been used to describe extensive struggles such as President Ronald Reagan's war on drugs and Prime Minister Brown's war on poverty. War implies aggressive conflict which will continue until either there is a winner or the parties concerned decide that a state of peace is preferable. With the advent of cyber war it has been suggested that the line between war and peace is becoming blurred.
War games (movie)	A 1983 Hollywood production describing how a teenage hacker can inadvertently cause a nuclear war scare.
Wargaming	In the military environment a war game may range from being a simple theoretical or hypothetical discussion, to a full-scale military exer-

Term	Definition
	cise involving troops and military equipment.
	In the academic cyberspace environment, wargaming is the process of simulating a war between two or more teams as a learning experience.
	In the video game world there are numerous products of the arcade game variety which have been described as war games.
Weakest link	By definition a system will almost invariably consist of a number of different components. Not all components will be of equal strength. The component which is most vulnerable to a cyber attack would be regarded as the weakest link. In the context of cyber warfare, it is often thought that the weakest link relates to people involved with the systems.
	See People problems.
Weaponized data	This is a wide-ranging issue as data can be weaponized in a number of different ways. It can be used to identify targets and to understand their vulnerabilities. This is how it is claimed Facebook data was used in the Cambridge Analytica scandal related to the presidential election in the USA in 2016.
	During this campaign it was suggested that data concerning the attitudes of candidates towards certain issues was sent to marginal voters with either the intention of encouraging them to support a particular candidate or in some cases to water down the resolve of certain voters to vote at all. In this way it is said that weaponized data was used in order to help win the election.

Term	Definition
Weaponized malware	Malicious software which has been designed to play a role in some cyber warfare activities. Almost any cyber device either hardware or software can be weaponized.
Web presence	If an individual engages in any activity with the Internet or the Web he or she is said to have a web presence. A more direct or specific web presence is a personal website or a profile with social media platforms such as Facebook, Twitter or Snapchat.
Web scraping	A form of data harvesting from websites. The data is collected from human readable sources. In this context the programs used are often referred to as bots or net bots and they collect information from often widely targeted entities on the web. The data so collected can be automatically presented in commonly used computer products such as a spreadsheet.
	This activity has also been described as large-scale data crawling and in general it is looked upon as being questionable from an ethical point of view.
	In some countries there is legislation prohibiting web scraping.
Web trail	A web trail is a record of user activity which shows which websites the user has been visiting. The term can also apply to organizations. It is similar to a digital shadow.
Webometrics	Webometrics measures aspects of the web with regard to the number and type of hyperlinks. It is an attempt to use quantitative methods to analyze information to make an assessment of how web content is designed and interrelated and

Term	Definition
	how it functions. The name Webometrics is also used for a website which ranks universities.
Website abuse	This term can have several different meanings. In the first case website abuse could refer to the use of a website to cause harm or offence to any individual or organization. On the other hand website abuse could be used to describe how a website has been changed by vandals or other individuals who wish to do harm to the web presence of an individual or organization.
Whatsapp	A free to download messenger app for smartphones. Similar to text messaging services, Whatsapp uses the internet to send messages, images, and audio or video. Because Whatsapp uses the internet to send messages, the cost is significantly less than texting. Whatsapp also offers end to end encryption
White hat	In cyberspace "white hat" refers to hackers who are directly employed by computer owners or agencies to test the vulnerability of their systems in order to discover any weaknesses and propose ways and means to minimize these potential problems.
Wifi Traffic	The amount of activity which is broadcast or received by devices connected to the Internet through WiFi. The amount of WiFi traffic affects the speed of any Internet activity, and thus varies considerably depending on the time of day.
Wiki	Server software that allows users to collaborate in forming the content of a website. The term comes from the word "wikiwiki," which means "fast" in the Hawaiian language. A wiki Web

Term	Definition
	site operates on a principle of collaborative trust. The simplest wiki programs allow users to create and edit content, whilst more advanced wikis have a management component that allow a designated person to moderate content. The best known example of a wiki website is Wikipedia.
Wikileaks	Founded in 2006 by Julian Assange, WikiLeaks is a website which contains information which had previously been regarded as confidential if not secret by one or other nation state. The objective of WikiLeaks is to embarrass nation states in the hope of making them more open with regards to the information they supply about the conduct of their affairs. This website has extensively offended almost everyone and it has resulted in its founder having to take refuge from international justice agencies in the embassy of the Republic of Ecuador in London. Among what WikiLeaks calls its co-publishers, research partners and funders are the New York Times, the Washington Post and the Wall Street Journal.
Wikimedia commons	A website which provides un-copyrighted (i.e. public domain) material which can be used by anyone in the production of articles books and videos etc. Wikimedia Commons is part of a growing movement which believes that copyright restrictions are sometimes too severe and hinders creativity.
Wikipedia	Launched in 2001 Wikipedia is a free, open access, cloud sourced encyclopedia which has been created and edited by volunteers from around the world. Wikipedia is available in

Term	Definition
	nearly 300 different languages. There are some 2 ½ million articles in the English version of Wikipedia. Wikipedia has often been challenged in terms of its accuracy but co-founder Jimmy Wales has suggested that there are no more errors in Wikipedia than there are in the Encyclopedia Britannica. It is hard to know how this assertion could be tested.
Wire tap	The surreptitious interception of any form of data, be it voice, text or graphics. In cyberspace a wiretap can be used to record transactions required for processing credit card purchases or debit card withdrawals or similar activities.
Worm	A worm is a computer virus which replicates itself and moves through a database altering or destroying data or software. A cyber worm will typically spread to other computers.

Z

Zero day exploit to Zombie computer

Term	Definition
Zero day exploit	This is a term used to indicate the day on which the producer or owner of a piece of software becomes aware of the specific vulnerability that is inherent in the software product being used. A zero day exploit is so named because there are zero days between when a vulnerability is discovered and when an attack to a system occurs.
Zombie computer	Also known as a Zombie bot, this is a computer that a remote attacker has accessed and set up to forward transmissions (including spam and viruses) to other computers on the Internet. The purpose is usually either financial gain or malice. Attackers typically exploit multiple computers to create a botnet, also known as a zombie army.

Link to website resources

Most of the terms in this glossary are supported by web links to articles, videos and other web content. To access these resources please click on the link below and fill out the short form.

http://academic-conferences.org/academic-publishing/cyber-links

Bibliography

Achohio, Byron and Jon Swartz. *Zero Day Threat,* Union Square Press, NY. (2008).

Akhgar, Babak, et al. *Cyber Crime and Cyber Terrorism: Investigator's Handbook,* Elsevier Syngress, Waltham, MA. (2014).

Akhgar, Babak, et al. eds. *Application of Big Data for National Security,* Elsevier, Waltham, MA. (2015).

Allhof, Fritz, Nisholas G. Evans and Adam Henschke. *Routledge Handbook of Ethics and War: Just War Theory in the 21st Century.* Routledge Handbooks, Routledge. (2015)

Alpaydin, Ethem. *Machine Learning.* The MIT Press. (2016)

Anderson R, "Why Cryptosystems Fail", *Communications of the ACM,* 37(11), pp32–40 (Nov 1994)

Anderson, R. (2013). *Security engineering.* Wiley, Hoboken, N.J.

Andress Jason and Steve Winterfield, *Cyber Warfare: Techniques, Tactics and Tools for Security Practitioners* 2nd ed. Syngress. (2013).

Andress, Jason, and Steve Winterfield. *Cyber Warfare: Techniques, Tactics and Tools for Security Practitioners.* : Syngress, Waltham. MA. (2011).

Andress, Jason. *The Basics of Information Security, 2nd ed.* Elsevier, Syngress, Waltham, MA. (2014).

Arquila, John and Douglas A. Boxer. *Information Strategy and Warfare,* Routledge, NY. (2007)

Atkinson, S., & Walker, C. (2015). *Psychology and the hacker – Psychological Incident.* SANS Institute InfoSec Reading Room.

Awan, Imran and Brian Blakemore. *Policing Cyber Hate, Cyber Threats and Cyber Terrorism,* Ashgate, Burlington. VT. (2012).

Barile. Ian, *Protecting Your PC*. Charles River Media Publisher, Boston, (2006).

Bayuk, Jennifer L, *Cyber Security Policy Guidebook*. Wiley. Hoboken, NJ, (2012)

Blackmore, Susan. *The Meme Machine*, Oxford University Press, (2000).

Bond M, "Attacks on Cryptoprocessor Transaction Sets" in *Proceedings of Workshop Cryptographic Hardware and Embedded Systems* (CHES 2001), LNCS 2162, Springer-Verlag, pp 220–234 (2001)

Brabham, Daren C, *Crowdsourcing*. The MIT Press. Cambridge MA.(2013).

Brenner, Joel. *America the Vulnerable: Inside the New Threat Matrix of Digital Espionage, Crime, and Warfare*. Penguin, New York, (2011).

Brenner, Susan W. *Cybercrime: Criminal Threats from Cyberspace*. Praeger. Santa Barbara, California. (2010). (See Chap. 4 *Target Cybercrimes: Hacking, Malware, and Distributed Denial of Service Attacks*).

Brenner, Susan W., *Cybercrime*. Praeger, Denver, Colorado. (2010).

Brodie, Bernard (1959), "8", *The Anatomy of Deterrence as found in Strategy in the Missile Age*, Princeton University Press, Princeton, pp. 264–304

Bucci, Steven, "Joining Cybercrime and Cyberterrorism: A Likely Scenario." in *CyberSpce and National Security: Threats, Opportunities, and Power in a Virtual World*. Ed. Derek S. Reveron. Georgetown University Press, Washington D.C. (2012).

Buckland, Michael. *Information and Society*. The MIT Press. Cambridge, MA. (2017).

Budka, Ph. and M. Kremser, (2004). "CyberAnthropology - Anthropology of CyberCulture", in S. Khittel, B. Plankensteiner and M. Six-Hohenbalken (eds.), *Contemporary issues in socio-cultural anthropology. Perspectives and research activities from Austria*, 213-226. Loecker, Vienna.

Bunz, Mercedes and Graham Meikle. *The Internet of Things,* Polity Press, UK. (2018)

Canetti D, Lindner M. Exposure to political violence and political behavior. In: Reynolds K, Branscombe N (eds), *Psychology of Change: Life Con-*

texts, Experiences, and Identities. Psychology Press, New York: (2014), pp. 77–94.

Capet, Philippe. *Information Evaluation,* Wiley, Hoboken, NJ. (2014).

Carr, Jeffrey, *Inside Cyber Warfare: Mapping the Cyber Underworld.* O'Reilly Media, Sebastopol, CA, (2009).

Carr, Jeffrey. *Inside Cyber Warfare: Mapping the Cyber Underworld.* O'Reilly Media, Sebastopol, CA, (2009).

Carty, Victoria, *Social Movement and New Technology.* Westview Press, Boulder, CO., (2015). (See Introduction The Digital Impact on Social Movements and Chap 4 Arab Spring).

Chapple Mike, Bill Ballad, Tricia Ballad and Erin K. Banks. *Access Control, Authentication, and Public Key Infrastructure,* 2ndEdn. Burlington, MA. 2014.

Chapple, Mike and David Seidl, *Cyberwarfare: Information Operations in a Connected World.* Jones and Barlett. (2015). (See: Chap. 9. *Defense-in-Depth Strategies,* Chap. 11. *Defending Endpoints,* Chap. 12. *Defending Networks,* and Chap. 13. *Defending Data*).

Chapple, Mike and David Seidl, *Cyberwarfare: Information Operations in a Connected World.* Jones and Bartlett. (2015). (See Chap. 2, *Targets and Combatants*).

Chapple, Mike and David Seidl, *Cyberwarfare: Information Operations in a Connected World.* Jones and Bartlett. (2015). (See Chap. 2. *Targets and Combatants*).

Chapple, Mike, and David Seidl, *Cyberwarfare: Information Operations in a Connected World.* Jones and Bartlett. (2015). (See Chap. 3. *Cyberwarfare, Law, and Ethics*).

Chapple, Mike, and David Seidl, *Cyberwarfare: Information Operations in a Connected World.* Jones and Bartlett. (2015). (See Chap. 2, *Targets and Combatants*).

Chapple, Mike, and David Seidl, *Cyberwarfare: Information Operations in a Connected World.* Jones and Bartlett. (2015). (See Chap. 5. *The Evolving Threat: From Script Kiddies to Advanced Attackers.* (The Cyber Kill Chain, pp. 107-121).

Chapple, Mike, and David Seidl, *Cyberwarfare: Information Operations in a Connected World.* Jones and Bartlett. (2015).

Chapple, Mike, and David Seidl, *Cyberwarfare: Information Operations in a Connected World.* Jones and Bartlett. (2015). (See Chap. 10. *Cryptography and Cyberwar*).

Chapple, Mike, and David Seidl, *Cyberwarfare: Information Operations in a Connected World.* Jones and Bartlett. (2015). (See Chap. 4. *Intelligence Operations in a Connected World*).

Chen, Hsinchun, *Dark Web: Exploring and Data Mining the Dark Side of the Web.* Springer, New York, (2012).

Clarke, Richard A. and Robert K. Knake. *Cyber War: The Threat to National Security and What to do About it.* Harper Collins, New York, (2010).

Coleman, Gabriella. Hacker, Hoaxer, Spy: The Many Faces of Anonymous. Verso, London, (2014)

Collman, Jeff and Sorin Adam Matei, eds., *Ethical Reasoning in Big Data.* Springer, Switzerland, (2016).

Cortada, James W. *Information and the Modern Corporation.* The MIT Press, Cambridge, MA. (2015).

Cyber Solutions. Global InfoTek, Inc. (GITI). Web. 30 Mar. (2011).

Day, Paul, *CyberAttack.* Carlton Books, London, (2013).

Deibert, Ronald J., *Black Code: Surveillance, Privacy, And The Dark Side of the Internet.* Signal Books, USA. (2013).

Denning, Dorothy E., *Information Warfare and Security.* Addison Wesley, New York, (1999). (See Chap. 5 Psyops and Perception Management).

Dijck, Jose Van. *The Culture of Connectivity: A Critical History of Social Media.* Oxford University Press, New York, (2013). (See Chap. 3 *Facebook and the Imperative of Sharing).*

Dijck, Jose Van. *The Culture of Connectivity: A Critical History of Social Media.* Oxford University Press, New York, (2013). (See Chap. 5 *Flickr between Communities and Commerce).*

Dinnis, Heather Harrison. *Cyber Warfare and the Laws of War.* Cambridge University Press, NY. (2012).

Doherty, Eamon P., *Digital Forensics for Handheld Devices.* CRC Press FL,. (2013).

Douglas, K. M. and R.M Sutton, (2011), "Does it take one to know one? Endorsement of Conspiracy Theories is Influenced by Personal Willingness to Conspire", *British Journal of Social Psychology*, 50, 544-52. doi:10.1111/j.2044-8309.

Dunham, Ken and Jim Melnick, *Malicious Bots: An Inside Look into the Cyber-criminal Underground of the Internet*. CRC Press, Boca Raton. Fl, (2009).

Duyvesteyn, Isabelle, "Between Doomsday and Dismissal: Cyber War, the Parameters of War, and Collective Defense." *Atlantisch Perspective* 38(7), (2014).

Engebretson, Patrick. *The Basics of Hacking and Penetration Testing, 2nd ed.* Elsevier, Syngress, Walthram, MA. (2013).

Esposito, John L and Natana J. DeLong-Bas. Shariah: *What Everyone Needs to Know*. Oxford University Press, New York, NY. (2018).

Ferguson, Andrew Guthrie, *The Rise of Big Data Policing*. New York University Press. New York, (2017).

Fidler, David P. ed. *The Snowden Reader*, Indiana University Press, Bloomington, Indianapolis. (2015).

Floridi, Luciano, ed., *Protection of Information and the Right to Privacy – A New Equilibrium?* Springer, NY. (2014).

Forest, James J. F. *Influence Warfare: How Terrorists and Governments Fight to Shape Perceptions in a War of Ideas*, Praeger Security International, Westport CT. (2009).

Fowler, Andrew, *The Most Dangerous Man in the World: The Explosive Story of Julian Assange and the Lies, Cover-ups and Conspiracies He Exposed*. Skyhorse, New York, (2011).

French, Shannon. *The Code of the Warrior*. Rowman & Littlefield Publishers, 2ed. (2016).

Frowe, Helen. *The Ethics of War and Peace*, 2nd ed. Routledge. (2015)

Gelvin, James, *The Arab Uprisings: What Everyone Needs To Know*, 2nd Ed. Oxford University Press. New York, NY. (2015).

Gelvin, James, *The New Middle East: What Everyone Needs to Know*. Oxford University Press. New York, NY. (2017)

Goglin, Greg. *Digital Forensics Explained*. CRC Press, Taylor & Francis Group. Boca Raton, Florida, (2013).

Goldfarb, Ronald, ed., *After Snowden,* St. Martin's Press, NY. (2015).

Gragido, Will and John Pirc, *Cybrtcrime and Espionage.* Syngress, Waltham, MA. (2011).

Gragido, Will et al. *Blackhatonomics. Syngress,* Waltham, MA. (2013).

Graham, David, "Cyber Threats and the Law of War." *Journal of National Security Law & Policy*. Vol. 4:87, (2010).

Grama, Joana Lyn, *Legal Issues in Information Security, 2nd ed.* Jones & Bartlett Learning (2015) (See Chap 3 *The American Legal System*).

Grama, Joana Lyn. *Legal Issues in Information Security, 2nd ed,* Jones & Bartlett Learning (2015) (See Chap 10 *Intellectual Property Law*)

Grama, Joana Lyn. Legal Issues in Information Security, 2nd ed, Jones & Bartlett Learning (2015) (See Chap 1 *Information Security Overview*).

Grama, Joana Lyn. *Legal Issues in Information Security*, 2nd ed. Jones & Bartlett Learning (2015) (See Chap 15 Computer Forensics and Investigations).

Grant, Tim. On the Military Geography of Cyberspace in Ryan, Julie, ed., *Leading Issues in Information Warfare & Security Research. Volume Two.* Academic Publishing International, United Kingdom. (2012). Pp. 119-138.

Greenberg, Andy, *This Machine Kills Secrets*: Julian Assange, the Cyperpunks, and Their fight to Empower Whistleblowers. Plume, New York, (2013)

Gunkel, David. *Hacking Cyberspace.* Westview Press, Boulder, Colorado. (2001).

Hables Gray, C. (2013). *Postmodern War*. Taylor and Francis. Florence

Hales D. and Patarin S. *How to cheat BitTorrent and why nobody does.* Technical Report UBLCS2005-12, University of Bologna, May (2005).

Harding, Luke. Collusion: Secret Meetings, Dirty Money, and How Russia Helped Trump Win, Vintage, NY. (2017).

Harris, Shane. *@War: The Rise of the Military-Internet Complex.* Houghton Mifflin Harcourt. NY. (2014).

Harrison Heather, *Cyber Warfare and the Laws of War.* Cambridge University Press. (2012).

Hasib Mansur, *Cybersecurity Leadership: Powering the Modern Organization*, CreateSpace Independent Publishing Platform. (2015).

Hawley, George, *Making Sense of The Alt-Right.* Columbia University Press. New York, NY. (2017).

Hawley, George, *The Alt Right: What Everyone Needs to Know.* Oxford Universty Press. New York NY, (2018).

Healey, Jason ed,. *A Fierce Domain: Conflict in Cyberspace, 1986 to 2012. Cyber Conflict Association Studies, (2013).*

Holt, Thomas J. *Crime On-line: Correlates, Causes, and Context, 2nd ed.* Carolina Academic Press, Durham, North Carolina, (2013). (See Chap 8 *Industrial Control Systems and Cyber crime.*)

Holt, Thomas J., *Crime On-line, 2nd ed.,* Carolina Academic Press, Durham, North Carolina. (2013).

Holt, Thomas, and Bernadette H. Schell. *Hackers and Hacking, ABC-CLIO,* Denver Colorado. (2013).

Holt. Thomas J., Adam M. Bossler and Kathryn C. Seigfried-Spellar. *CyberCrime and Digital Forensics.* Routledge, London and New York, (2015). (See Chap. 5 *Economic crimes and online fraud*).

Holt. Thomas J., Adam M. Bossler and Kathryn C. Seigfried-Spellar. *CyberCrime and Digital Forensics.* Routledge, London and New York, (2015). (See Chap. 7 *Cyberbullying, online harassment and cyber stalking*).

Holt. Thomas J., Adam M. Bossler and Kathryn C. Seigfried-Spellar. *CyberCrime and Digital Forensics.* Routledge, London and New York, (2015). (See Chap. 7 *Cyberbullying, online harassment and cyber stalking*).

Holt. Thomas J., Adam M. Bossler, and Kathryn C. Seigfried-Spellar, *CyberCrime and Digital Forensics.* Routledge. London and New York, (2015), (See Chap. 9 *Cybercrime and criminological theories*).

Holt. Thomas J., Adam M. Bossler, and Kathryn C. Seigfried-Spellar. *CyberCrime and Digital Forensics. ,* Routledge, London and New York. (2015). (See Chap. 10 *Evolution of digital forensics*).

Holt. Thomas J., Adam M. Bossler, and Kathryn C. Seigfried-Spellar. *CyberCrime and Digital Forensics*. Routledge, London and New York, (2015). (See Chap. 5 *Economic crimes and online fraud*).

Holt. Thomas J., Adam M. Bossler, and Kathryn C. Seigfried-Spellar. *CyberCrime and Digital Forensics*. Routledge. London and New York, (2015). (See Chap. 8 *Online extremism, cyberterror, and cyber warfare*).

Hughes, Rex B, "NATO and CyberDefence, Mission Accomplished?" *Atlantisch Perspective* 33(1), (2009).

James, Bradley & Fletcher, Bobbie. (2015). Understanding the Fanboy Culture; Their Place and Role within the Games Industry. https://www.researchgate.net/publication/299398285.

Jewkes Yvonne and Majid Yar, *Handbook of Internet Crime*. Willan Publishing. London, (2010).

Johnson, Thomas A. ed., *Cybersecurity: Protecting Critical Infrastructures From Cyber Attack and Cyber Warfare.* CRC Press. Taylor & Francis Group, New York, (2015). (See Chap. 2 *Critical Infrastructures, Key Assets: A Target-Rich Environment* and Chap. 3 *Protection and Engineering Design Issues in Critical infrastructures.*)

Johnson, Thomas A. ed., *Cybersecurity: Protecting Critical infrastructures From Cyber Attack and Cyber Warfare.* CRC Press. Taylor & Francis Group, New York, (2015). (See Chap. 4 *Cyber Intelligence, Cyber Conflicts, and Cyber Warfare*).

Johnson, Thomas A. ed., *Cybersecurity: Protecting Critical infrastructures From Cyber Attack and Cyber Warfare.* CRC Press. Taylor & Francis Group. New York, (2015).

Johnson, Thomas A. ed., *Cybersecurity: Protecting Critical infrastructures From Cyber Attack and Cyber Warfare.* CRC Press. Taylor & Francis Group. New York, (2015). (See Chap 6 *Economic Cost of Cybersecurity*).

Johnson, Thomas A., ed. *Cybersecurity: Protecting Critical Infrastructures from Cyber Attack and Cyber Warfare.* CRC Press, Boca Raton, FL: (2015).

Jordan, Tim and Paul Taylor. *Hacktivism and Cyberwars: Rebels with a Cause?* Routledge. (2004).

Jordan, Tim. *Hacking: Digital Media and Technological Determinism,* Polity Press, Medford, MA. (2008).

Kaplan, Jerry, *Artificial Intelligence: What Everyone Wants to Know.* New York, NY. (2016).

Kello, Lucas, *The Virtual Weapon and the International Order.* Yale University Press, New Haven, CT. (2017).

Khader, Majeed, Loo Seng Neo, Gabriel Ong, Eunice Tan Mingyi, and Jeffrey Chin. *Combatting Violent Extremism and Radicalization in the Digital Era.* IGI Global. (2016)

Kirwan G and Andrea Power *The Psychology of Cyber Crime: Concepts and Principles.* IGI Global Publishing. (2011).

Kirwan, G., & Power, A. (2013). *Cybercrime: Psychology of cybercrime. Dublin*: Dun Laoghaire Institute of Art, Design and Technology.

Klimburg, Alexander. *The Darkening Web: The War for Cyberspace.* Penguin Press, NY. (2017).

Kostopoulos, George K. *Cyberspace and Cybersecurity.* CRC Press, NY. (2013).

Krutz, Ronald. *Securing SCADA Systems.* Wiley, Hoboken, NJ. (2006).

Le Pichon, A., J. Vergoz, P. Herry and L. Ceranna (2008), "Analyzing the detection capability of infrasound arrays in central Europe", *Journal of Geophysics Research*, 113, D12115, doi:10.1029/2007JD009509.

Lee, Newton. *Facebook Nation, 2nd ed.,* New York, Springer. (2014). (See Chap 11 *E-Government and E-Activism* and Chap 9 *Misinformation and Disinformation)*

Lee, Newton. *Facebook Nation, 2nd ed.,* New York, Springer. (2014). (See Chap 11 *E-Government and E-Activi*sm and Chap 9 *Misinformation and Disinformation)*

Lee, Newton. *Facebook Nation, 2nd ed.,* Springer, New York, (2014). (See Chap 11 *E-Government and E-Activism*)

Lee, Newton. *Facebook Nation, 2nd ed.,* Springer. New York, (2014). (See Chap 11 *E-Government and E-Activism*).

Lee, Newton. *Facebook Nation, 2nd ed.,* Springer. New York, (2014).

Lee, Wenke, Cliff Wang and David Dagon. *Botnet Detection: Countering the Largest Security Threat.* Springer, New York, (2008).

Lehto, Martti, and Pekka Neittssnmaki. *Cyber Security: Analytics, Technology and Aiutomation.* Springer, (2015).

Levine, Yasha. *Surveillance Valley: The Secret Military History of the Internet.* Public Affairs, NY. (2018).

Libicki, Martin C, *Cyber Deterrence and Cyber War.* Monograph, RAND Corporation, Arlington, (2009).

Libicki, Martin C, *Cyberspace in Peace and War.* Naval Institute Press. Annnapolis, Maryland, (2016). (See Chap. 23 *Attribution*).

Libicki, Martin, *Crisis and Escalation in Cyberspace.* RAND, Santa Monica, CA, (2012).

Libicki, Martin, *Cyberdeterrence and Cyberwarfare.* RAND, Santa Monica, CA. (2009).

Libicki, Martin. *Cyberspace in Peace and War.* Annapolis. MD: U. S. Naval Academy. (2016).

Libicki, Martin. *Cyberspace in Peace and War.* Naval Academy Press, Annapolis, MD, U.S. (2016).

Lindsay, Jon R., Tai Ming Cheung and Derek S Reveron, Eds. *China and Cybersecurity: Espionage, Strategy, and Politics in the Digital Domain.* Oxford University Press, New York, (2015).

Loukas, George. *Cyber-Physical Attacks, Elsevier, Waltham, MA.* (2015).

Lucas G R. State sponsored hacktivism. In: Gross M L, Meisels T. (eds), *Soft War, the Ethics of Unarmed Conflict.* Cambridge University Press, Cambridge: (2017).

Lucas, George. *Military Ethics: What Everyone Needs to Know.*Oxford University Press, New York, NY. (2016).

Lucas, George. *Ethics and Cyber Warfare: The Quest for Responsible Security in the Age of Digital Warfare.* Oxford University Press. New York, NY. (2016).

Mahmood, Zaigham, ed. *Continued Rise of the Cloud: Advances and Trends in Cloud Computing.* Springer, London, (2014).

Mandiant Corporation. *APT1: Exposing One of China's Cyber Espionage Units.* Mandiant Corporation, Alexandria, VA (2013).

Manjikian, Mary. *Deterring Cybertrespass and securing Cyberspace: Lessons form United States Border Control Stra*tegies. CreateSpace Independent Publishing Platform, (2017).

Marteau TM, Bekker H, "The development of a Six-Item Short-Form of the State Scale of the Spielberger State - Trait Anxiety Inventory (STAI)". *British Journal of Clinical Psychology* (1992) 31:301–306.

Mayer-Schonberger, Viktor and Kenneth Cukier, *Big Data*. Houghton Mifflin Harcourt, New York, (2013).

Mayer-Schonberger, Viktor and Kenneth Cukier. *Big Data: A Revolution That Will Transform How We Live, Work, and Think*. Houghton Mifflin Harcourt, NY. (2013).

Mazanec, Brian M. and Bradley A. Thayer, *Deterring Cyber warfare*. Palgrave, Macmillan, New York, (2015).

McClure, Stuart & Scambray, Joel & Kurtz, George. *Hacking Exposed: Network Security Secrets and Solutions* McGraw Hill Professional Publishing, (1999).

McGee, Joshua, *NATO and Cyber Defense: A Brief Overview and Recent Events*. Center for Strategic & International Studies, July 8. (2011).

McGuire, Michael. "Child pornography," in Jewkes Yvonne and Majid Yar, *Handbook of Internet Crime*, chap. 17. Willan Publishing, London, (2010). Pp. 343-368.

McGuire, Michael. "Online surveillance and personal liberty," in Jewkes Yvonne and Majid Yar, *Handbook of Internet Crime*, Chap. 23. Willan Publishing, London, (2010). Pp. 492-519.

McMahan, Jeff. *Killing in War*. Oxford University Press. (2011)

Middleton, Bruce. *A History of Cyber Security Attacks: 1980 to Present*. CRC Press, Taylor and Francis Group. Boca Raton, FL. (2017).

Nagle, Angela, *Kill All Normies: Online Culture Wars from 4Chan and Tumblr to Trump and the Alt Right*. Zero books, Washington, US. (2017).

Nance, Malcom. *The Plot to Hack America*. Skyhorse Publishing, New York, (2016).

NATO Parliamentary Assembly, *NATO and Cyber Defence. 2009 Annual Session*. Brussels, (2009).

Netanel, *Copyright: What Everyone Needs to Know*. Oxford University Press, New York, NY. (2018)

Nilsson, Nils J. *The Quest For Artificial Intelligence. Cambridge University Press.* (2010).

Obama, Barack. *The Comprehensive National Cybersecurity Initiative.* White House, Washington. D.C. (2009).

Olsen, Parmi. *We are Anonymous: Inside the Hacker World of LulzSec, Anonymous and the Global Cyber Insurgency.* Black Bay Books, New York (2012).

Orend, Brian. *The Morality of War, 2nd ed.*, Broadview Press, (2013).

Oriyano, Sean-Phillip, *Hacker Techniques, Tools, and Incident Handling,* 2nd ed.,Jones and Bartlett, Burlington, MA. (2014). (See Chap. 15 *Defensive Technologies*).

Oriyano, Sean-Phillip. *Hacker Techniques, Tools, and Incident Handling,* 2nd ed.,Jones and Bartlett, Burlington, MA. (2014). (See Chap. 9 *Web and Database Attacks*).

Oriyano, Sean-Phillip. *Hacker Techniques, Tools, and Incident Handling, 2nd edn.* Jones and Bartlett, Burlington, MA. (2014) *(*See Chap. 1 *Hacking The Next Generation. 2014).*

Oriyano, Sean-Phillip. *Hacker Techniques, Tools, and Incident Handling, 2nd ed.,*Jones and Bartlett, Burlington, MA. (2014). (See Chap. 10 *Malware*).

Osborne, Mark. *Cyberattack, Cybercrime, Cyberwarfare: Cybercomplacency*, CreateSpace Independent Publishing Platform, North Charleston, South Carolina. (2013) (See Chap. 2 *The Internet is a Business – Understanding the E-Economy Platform*, pp. 13-30).

Panghorn, DJ. Aaron Swartz's 'Guerilla Open Access Manifesto' Is More Important Than Ever. *Mother Board Blog*, August 14, (2013). https://motherboard.vice.com/en_us/article/bmm958/aaron-swartz-guerilla-open-access-manifesto-is-more-important-than-ever

Parno, Bryan, "Trust Extension as a Mechanism for Secure Code Execution on Commodity Computers" (2010). *Dissertations. Paper* 28.

Poibeau, Thierry. *Machine Translation.* The MIT Press. Cambridge, MA.(2017)

Pomerantz, Jeffrey. *Metadata.*), The Mit Press, Cambridge, MA. (2015).

Poroshyn, Roman. *Stuxnet: The True Story of Hunt and Evolution.* Outskirts Press, Denver, CO. (2013).

Reck, Robb, *Defense in Depth Is Necessary, but Not Sufficient.* InfoReck. Web. 30 Mar. (2011).

Regalado, Daniel, Shon Harris. Allen Harper, Chris Eagle, Jonathan Ness. Branko Spasojevic, Ryan Lin, and Stephen Sims. *Gray Hat Hacking, 4th ed.* McGraw Hill Education, New York, (2015).

Rosenzwaig, Paul, *Cyber Warfare.* Santa Barbara: California. Praeger, (2013). (See Chap, 8 *Cyber Conflict and The Constitution*).

Rosenzwaig, Paul, *Cyber Warfare.* Santa Barbara: Praeger, California. (2013). (See Chap. 4 *Cyber War and the Law* and Chap. 7 *Cybercrime*).

Rosenzwaig, Paul. *Cyber Warfare.* Praeger, Santa Barbara, California, (2013).

Rosenzwaig, Paul. *Cyber Warfare.* Praeger, Santa Barbara, California. (2013). (See Chap. 12, *Encryption and Wiretapping*).

Rosenzwaig, Paul. *Cyber Warfare.* Praeger, Santa Barbara: California: (2013). (See Chap. 5 *Cyber-Insurgency*).

Rowe, Neil C. and Julian Rrushi. *Introduction to Cyberdeception.* Springer International Publishing. Switzerland, (2016).

Ruparella, Nayan B, *Cloud Computing.* The MIT Press, Cambridge, MA. (2016).

Ryan, Julie, ed. *Leading Issues in Information Warfare & Security Research, Vol. 1,* Academic Publishing International Limited, Reading, UK. (2012).

Ryan, Julie. *Leading Issues in Information Warfare & Security, Vol. 2,* Academic Conferences and Publishing International Limited, Reading, UK. (2015).

Sandler, Todd. *Terrorism: What Everyone Needs to Know*, Oxford University Press, New York, NY. (2018).

Satapathy C, "Impact of Cyber Vandalism on the Internet", *Economic and Political Weekly*, Vol. 35, No. 13 Mar. 25-31, (2000), pp. 1059-1061, Published by: Economic and Political Weekly, Stable URL: http://www.jstor.org/stable/4409073

Schmitt, Michael, "Classification of Cyber Conflict." *Journal of Conflict & Security Law*. Vol 12 (2), (2012).

Schmitt, Michael, N., *Tallinn Manual on the International Law Applicable to Cyber Warfare*. Cambridge University Press, New York, (2013).

Schmitt, Michael, N., *Tallinn Manual on the International Law Applicable to Cyber Warfare*. Cambridge University Press, New York: (2013).

Schneider, Bruce, *Secrets and Lies: Digital Security in a Digital World*. John Wiley & Sons, Inc., New York, (2000).

Schneier, Bruce. *Secrets and Lies: Digital Security in a Networked World,* Wiley Publishing, Inc., Indianapolis, Indiana. (2000).

Sifry, Micah L. *Wikileaks and the Age of Transparency,* Counterpoint Press, Berkeley, CA. (2011).

Simpson, C. (2015). *Science of coercion*. Open Road Integrated Media, New York.

Singer, P. W. and Allan Friedman. *Cybersecurity and Cyber War: What Everyone Should Know*. Oxford University Press, New York, (2014).

Skinnell, Ryan, ed. *Faking The News,* Societas, UK. (2018).

Smith S. W. and S. Weingart, "Building a high-performance, programmable secure coprocessor". *Computer Networks*, 31(8), Apr. (1999). (Referenced on pages 17, 25, 32, 46, and 60.)

Smith, Russell G. "Identity Theft and fraud," in Jewkes Yvonne and Majid Yar, *Handbook of Internet Crime,* Chap.14. Willan Publishing. London, (2010). Pp. 273-301.

Solomon, Alan, *PC Viruses: Detection, Analysis, and Crime.* Springer-Verlag, London, (1991).

Stryker, Cole. *Epic Win For Anonymous: How 4Chan's Army Conquered The Web,* Overlook Duckworth, NY. (2011).

Suber, Peter. *Open Access,* The MIT Press, Cambridge, MA.(2012).

Talbot Jensen Eric, "Cyber Attacks: Proportionality and Precautions" in *Attack*, 89 INT'L. L. STUD. 198, 200–01 (2013).(discussing differing viewpoints).

Tapscott, Don, and Alex Tapscott, *Blockchain Revolution: How the Technology behind Bitcoin Is Changing Money, Business, and the World.* Penguin, (2016).

Taxonomy of the Computer Security Incident Related Terminology.
TERENA. Web. 20 Mar. (2011).

Tsetsura, Katerina and Dean Kruckeberg. *Transparency, Public Relations, and The Mass Media*, Routledge, NY. (2017).

Tsirigotis, Alexander. Cyber Warfare: Virtual war Among Virtual Societies in Ryan, Julie, ed., *Leading Issues in Information Warfare & Security Research*. Volume One. Academic Publishing International, UK, (2012).

Ullah, Haroon K. *Digital World War,* Yale University Press. New Haven, CT. (2017).

Ventra, Daniel. *Information Warfare.* Hoboken, N.J. Wiley, (2009).

Ventre, Daniel. *Information Warfare 2nd ed,* Wiley, Hoboken, NJ. (2016).

Vigna, Paul, and Michael J. Casey, *The Age of Cryptocurrency: How Bitcoin and the Blockchain are Challenging the Global Economic Order*. St. Martin's Press, New York, (2015).

Walzer, Michael. *Just and Unjust War: A Moral Argument with Historical Illustrations,* 4th ed. Basic Books, New York. (2015).

Wareham, Allen and Steve Furnell. Electronic Activism: Threats, Implications and Responses, in Ryan, Julie, ed., *Leading Issues in Information Warfare & Security Research. Volume Two*. Academic Publishing International . United Kingdom, (2012). Pp. 132-147.

Warren, Matthew. *Case Studies in Information Warfare and Security.* Academic Conferences and Publishing International Limited, Reading, UK. (2013).

Weimann, Gabriel, *Terrorism in Cyberspace.* Woodrow Wilson Center Press, Washington, D. C. (2015).

Weimann,Gabriel, *Terror on the Internet.* United States Institute of Peace, Washington, D. C. , (2006).